Contact Informat

MW00885670

Full Name: _____

Address: _____

_____

Email: _____

Phone: _____

_____

Start Date: _____

End Date: _____

Signer Full NAME:		Phone No:		Record No:	

Address:		Email:	Thumb Print:

Service Performed	Identification	ID Number:	Issued by:	Signature:
☐ Acknowledgement	☐ ID Card			
☐ Jurat	☐ Driver's License	**Issued Date:**	**Expiration Date:**	
☐ Oath	☐ Passport	/ /	/ /	
Other:	☐ Credible Witness	**Document Date:**	**Notary Fee:**	**Travel Fee:**
	☐ Known Personally	/ /		
	☐ _____			

Document Type:	Date/Time Notarized: / /	:	AM
		:	PM

Witness Full NAME: 1	Signature:	Phone No:
Address:		Email:
Witness Full NAME: 2	Signature:	Phone No:
Address:		Email:

Notes:

Signer Full NAME:		Phone No:		Record No:	

Address:		Email:	Thumb Print:

Service Performed	Identification	ID Number:	Issued by:	Signature:
☐ Acknowledgement	☐ ID Card			
☐ Jurat	☐ Driver's License	**Issued Date:**	**Expiration Date:**	
☐ Oath	☐ Passport	/ /	/ /	
Other:	☐ Credible Witness	**Document Date:**	**Notary Fee:**	**Travel Fee:**
	☐ Known Personally	/ /		
	☐ _____			

Document Type:	Date/Time Notarized: / /	:	AM
		:	PM

Witness Full NAME: 1	Signature:	Phone No:
Address:		Email:
Witness Full NAME: 2	Signature:	Phone No:
Address:		Email:

Notes:

Signer Full NAME:		Phone No:		Record No:	

Address:		Email:		Thumb Print:

Service Performed	Identification	ID Number:	Issued by:	Signature:	
☐ Acknowledgement ☐ Jurat ☐ Oath Other:	☐ ID Card ☐ Driver's License ☐ Passport ☐ Credible Witness ☐ Known Personally ☐ _____	Issued Date: / /	Expiration Date: / /		
		Document Date: / /	Notary Fee:	Travel Fee:	

Document Type:	Date/Time Notarized: / /	: AM : PM

Witness Full NAME: 1	Signature:	Phone No:
Address:		Email:
Witness Full NAME: 2	Signature:	Phone No:
Address:		Email:

Notes:

Signer Full NAME:		Phone No:		Record No:	

Address:		Email:		Thumb Print:

Service Performed	Identification	ID Number:	Issued by:	Signature:	
☐ Acknowledgement ☐ Jurat ☐ Oath Other:	☐ ID Card ☐ Driver's License ☐ Passport ☐ Credible Witness ☐ Known Personally ☐ _____	Issued Date: / /	Expiration Date: / /		
		Document Date: / /	Notary Fee:	Travel Fee:	

Document Type:	Date/Time Notarized: / /	: AM : PM

Witness Full NAME: 1	Signature:	Phone No:
Address:		Email:
Witness Full NAME: 2	Signature:	Phone No:
Address:		Email:

Notes:

Signer Full NAME:		Phone No:		Record No:	
Address:			Email:		Thumb Print:

Service Performed	Identification	ID Number:	Issued by:	Signature:
☐ Acknowledgement ☐ Jurat ☐ Oath Other:	☐ ID Card ☐ Driver's License ☐ Passport ☐ Credible Witness ☐ Known Personally ☐ _____	**Issued Date:** / /	**Expiration Date:** / /	
		Document Date: / /	**Notary Fee:**	**Travel Fee:**

Document Type:	Date/Time Notarized: / /	: AM : PM

Witness Full NAME: 1	Signature:	Phone No:
Address:		Email:
Witness Full NAME: 2	Signature:	Phone No:
Address:		Email:

Notes:

Signer Full NAME:		Phone No:		Record No:	
Address:			Email:		Thumb Print:

Service Performed	Identification	ID Number:	Issued by:	Signature:
☐ Acknowledgement ☐ Jurat ☐ Oath Other:	☐ ID Card ☐ Driver's License ☐ Passport ☐ Credible Witness ☐ Known Personally ☐ _____	**Issued Date:** / /	**Expiration Date:** / /	
		Document Date: / /	**Notary Fee:**	**Travel Fee:**

Document Type:	Date/Time Notarized: / /	: AM : PM

Witness Full NAME: 1	Signature:	Phone No:
Address:		Email:
Witness Full NAME: 2	Signature:	Phone No:
Address:		Email:

Notes:

Signer Full NAME:		Phone No:		Record No:	

Address: | **Email:** | **Thumb Print:**

Service Performed	Identification	ID Number:	Issued by:	Signature:
☐ Acknowledgement ☐ Jurat ☐ Oath Other:	☐ ID Card ☐ Driver's License ☐ Passport ☐ Credible Witness ☐ Known Personally ☐ _____	**Issued Date:** / /	**Expiration Date:** / /	
		Document Date: / /	**Notary Fee:**	**Travel Fee:**

Document Type:	Date/Time Notarized: / /	: AM : PM

Witness Full NAME: 1	Signature:	Phone No:
Address:		Email:
Witness Full NAME: 2	Signature:	Phone No:
Address:		Email:

Notes:

Signer Full NAME:		Phone No:		Record No:	

Address: | **Email:** | **Thumb Print:**

Service Performed	Identification	ID Number:	Issued by:	Signature:
☐ Acknowledgement ☐ Jurat ☐ Oath Other:	☐ ID Card ☐ Driver's License ☐ Passport ☐ Credible Witness ☐ Known Personally ☐ _____	**Issued Date:** / /	**Expiration Date:** / /	
		Document Date: / /	**Notary Fee:**	**Travel Fee:**

Document Type:	Date/Time Notarized: / /	: AM : PM

Witness Full NAME: 1	Signature:	Phone No:
Address:		Email:
Witness Full NAME: 2	Signature:	Phone No:
Address:		Email:

Notes:

Signer Full NAME:		Phone No:		Record No:

Address:		Email:		Thumb Print:

Service Performed	Identification	ID Number:	Issued by:	Signature:
☐ Acknowledgement	☐ ID Card			
☐ Jurat	☐ Driver's License	Issued Date:	Expiration Date:	
☐ Oath	☐ Passport	/ /	/ /	
Other:	☐ Credible Witness	Document Date:	Notary Fee:	Travel Fee:
	☐ Known Personally			
	☐ _____	/ /		

Document Type:	Date/Time Notarized: / /	: AM
		: PM

Witness Full NAME: 1	Signature:	Phone No:
Address:		Email:

Witness Full NAME: 2	Signature:	Phone No:
Address:		Email:

Notes:

Signer Full NAME:		Phone No:		Record No:

Address:		Email:		Thumb Print:

Service Performed	Identification	ID Number:	Issued by:	Signature:
☐ Acknowledgement	☐ ID Card			
☐ Jurat	☐ Driver's License	Issued Date:	Expiration Date:	
☐ Oath	☐ Passport	/ /	/ /	
Other:	☐ Credible Witness	Document Date:	Notary Fee:	Travel Fee:
	☐ Known Personally			
	☐	/ /		

Document Type:	Date/Time Notarized: / /	: AM
		: PM

Witness Full NAME: 1	Signature:	Phone No:
Address:		Email:

Witness Full NAME: 2	Signature:	Phone No:
Address:		Email:

Notes:

Signer Full NAME:		Phone No:		Record No:
Address:		Email:		Thumb Print:

Service Performed	Identification	ID Number:	Issued by:	Signature:
☐ Acknowledgement ☐ Jurat ☐ Oath Other:	☐ ID Card ☐ Driver's License ☐ Passport ☐ Credible Witness ☐ Known Personally ☐	Issued Date: / /	Expiration Date: / /	
		Document Date: / /	Notary Fee:	Travel Fee:

Document Type:	Date/Time Notarized: / /	: AM : PM

Witness Full NAME: 1	Signature:	Phone No:
Address:		Email:
Witness Full NAME: 2	Signature:	Phone No:
Address:		Email:

Notes:

Signer Full NAME:		Phone No:		Record No:
Address:		Email:		Thumb Print:

Service Performed	Identification	ID Number:	Issued by:	Signature:
☐ Acknowledgement ☐ Jurat ☐ Oath Other:	☐ ID Card ☐ Driver's License ☐ Passport ☐ Credible Witness ☐ Known Personally ☐	Issued Date: / /	Expiration Date: / /	
		Document Date: / /	Notary Fee:	Travel Fee:

Document Type:	Date/Time Notarized: / /	: AM : PM

Witness Full NAME: 1	Signature:	Phone No:
Address:		Email:
Witness Full NAME: 2	Signature:	Phone No:
Address:		Email:

Notes:

Signer Full NAME:		Phone No:		Record No:
Address:		Email:		Thumb Print:

Service Performed	Identification	ID Number:	Issued by:	Signature:
☐ Acknowledgement ☐ Jurat ☐ Oath Other:	☐ ID Card ☐ Driver's License ☐ Passport ☐ Credible Witness ☐ Known Personally ☐ _____	Issued Date: / / Document Date: / /	Expiration Date: / / Notary Fee:	Travel Fee:

Document Type:	Date/Time Notarized: / /	: AM : PM

Witness Full NAME: 1	Signature:	Phone No:
Address:		Email:
Witness Full NAME: 2	Signature:	Phone No:
Address:		Email:

Notes:

Signer Full NAME:		Phone No:		Record No:
Address:		Email:		Thumb Print:

Service Performed	Identification	ID Number:	Issued by:	Signature:
☐ Acknowledgement ☐ Jurat ☐ Oath Other:	☐ ID Card ☐ Driver's License ☐ Passport ☐ Credible Witness ☐ Known Personally ☐ _____	Issued Date: / / Document Date: / /	Expiration Date: / / Notary Fee:	Travel Fee:

Document Type:	Date/Time Notarized: / /	: AM : PM

Witness Full NAME: 1	Signature:	Phone No:
Address:		Email:
Witness Full NAME: 2	Signature:	Phone No:
Address:		Email:

Notes:

Signer Full NAME:	Phone No:	Record No:

Address:	Email:	Thumb Print:

Service Performed	Identification	ID Number:	Issued by:	Signature:

□ Acknowledgement
□ Jurat
□ Oath
Other:
	□ ID Card
	□ Driver's License
	□ Passport
	□ Credible Witness
	□ Known Personally
	□ _____
		Issued Date:
		  / /
			Expiration Date:
			  / /	

		Document Date: / /	Notary Fee:	Travel Fee:

Document Type:	Date/Time Notarized: / /	: AM
		: PM

Witness Full NAME: 1	Signature:	Phone No:
Address:		Email:
Witness Full NAME: 2	Signature:	Phone No:
Address:		Email:

Notes:

Signer Full NAME:	Phone No:	Record No:

Address:	Email:	Thumb Print:

Service Performed	Identification	ID Number:	Issued by:	Signature:

□ Acknowledgement
□ Jurat
□ Oath
Other:
	□ ID Card
	□ Driver's License
	□ Passport
	□ Credible Witness
	□ Known Personally
	□ _____
		Issued Date:
		  / /
			Expiration Date:
			  / /	

		Document Date: / /	Notary Fee:	Travel Fee:

Document Type:	Date/Time Notarized: / /	: AM
		: PM

Witness Full NAME: 1	Signature:	Phone No:
Address:		Email:
Witness Full NAME: 2	Signature:	Phone No:
Address:		Email:

Notes:

Record 1

Signer Full NAME: | **Phone No:** | **Record No:**

Address: | **Email:** | **Thumb Print:**

Service Performed	Identification	ID Number:	Issued by:	Signature:
□ Acknowledgement	□ ID Card			
□ Jurat	□ Driver's License	**Issued Date:**	**Expiration Date:**	
□ Oath	□ Passport	/ /	/ /	
Other:	□ Credible Witness	**Document Date:**	**Notary Fee:**	**Travel Fee:**
	□ Known Personally	/ /		
	□ _____			

Document Type: | **Date/Time Notarized:** / / | : AM |
| | : PM |

Witness Full NAME: 1	Signature:	Phone No:
Address:		Email:
Witness Full NAME: 2	Signature:	Phone No:
Address:		Email:

Notes:

Record 2

Signer Full NAME: | **Phone No:** | **Record No:**

Address: | **Email:** | **Thumb Print:**

Service Performed	Identification	ID Number:	Issued by:	Signature:
□ Acknowledgement	□ ID Card			
□ Jurat	□ Driver's License	**Issued Date:**	**Expiration Date:**	
□ Oath	□ Passport	/ /	/ /	
Other:	□ Credible Witness	**Document Date:**	**Notary Fee:**	**Travel Fee:**
	□ Known Personally	/ /		
	□			

Document Type: | **Date/Time Notarized:** / / | : AM |
| | : PM |

Witness Full NAME: 1	Signature:	Phone No:
Address:		Email:
Witness Full NAME: 2	Signature:	Phone No:
Address:		Email:

Notes:

Signer Full NAME:		Phone No:		Record No:	

Address:		Email:		Thumb Print:

Service Performed	Identification	ID Number:	Issued by:	Signature:
☐ Acknowledgement	☐ ID Card			
☐ Jurat	☐ Driver's License	**Issued Date:**	**Expiration Date:**	
☐ Oath	☐ Passport	/ /	/ /	
Other:	☐ Credible Witness	**Document Date:**	**Notary Fee:**	**Travel Fee:**
	☐ Known Personally	/ /		
	☐ _____			

Document Type:	Date/Time Notarized: / /	: AM
		: PM

Witness Full NAME: 1	Signature:	Phone No:
Address:		Email:
Witness Full NAME: 2	Signature:	Phone No:
Address:		Email:

Notes:

Signer Full NAME:		Phone No:		Record No:	

Address:		Email:		Thumb Print:

Service Performed	Identification	ID Number:	Issued by:	Signature:
☐ Acknowledgement	☐ ID Card			
☐ Jurat	☐ Driver's License	**Issued Date:**	**Expiration Date:**	
☐ Oath	☐ Passport	/ /	/ /	
Other:	☐ Credible Witness	**Document Date:**	**Notary Fee:**	**Travel Fee:**
	☐ Known Personally	/ /		
	☐ _____			

Document Type:	Date/Time Notarized: / /	: AM
		: PM

Witness Full NAME: 1	Signature:	Phone No:
Address:		Email:
Witness Full NAME: 2	Signature:	Phone No:
Address:		Email:

Notes:

Signer Full NAME:		Phone No:		Record No:
Address:			Email:	Thumb Print:

Service Performed	Identification	ID Number:	Issued by:	Signature:
☐ Acknowledgement ☐ Jurat ☐ Oath Other:	☐ ID Card ☐ Driver's License ☐ Passport ☐ Credible Witness ☐ Known Personally ☐ _____	Issued Date: / / Document Date: / /	Expiration Date: / / Notary Fee:	Travel Fee:

Document Type:	Date/Time Notarized: / /	: AM : PM

Witness Full NAME: 1	Signature:	Phone No:
Address:		Email:
Witness Full NAME: 2	Signature:	Phone No:
Address:		Email:

Notes:

Signer Full NAME:		Phone No:		Record No:
Address:			Email:	Thumb Print:

Service Performed	Identification	ID Number:	Issued by:	Signature:
☐ Acknowledgement ☐ Jurat ☐ Oath Other:	☐ ID Card ☐ Driver's License ☐ Passport ☐ Credible Witness ☐ Known Personally ☐ _____	Issued Date: / / Document Date: / /	Expiration Date: / / Notary Fee:	Travel Fee:

Document Type:	Date/Time Notarized: / /	: AM : PM

Witness Full NAME: 1	Signature:	Phone No:
Address:		Email:
Witness Full NAME: 2	Signature:	Phone No:
Address:		Email:

Notes:

Signer Full NAME:		Phone No:		Record No:	
Address:			Email:		Thumb Print:

Service Performed	Identification	ID Number:	Issued by:	Signature:	
☐ Acknowledgement	☐ ID Card				
☐ Jurat	☐ Driver's License	Issued Date:	Expiration Date:		
☐ Oath	☐ Passport	/ /	/ /		
Other:	☐ Credible Witness	Document Date:	Notary Fee:	Travel Fee:	
	☐ Known Personally	/ /			
	☐				

Document Type:	Date/Time Notarized: / /	: AM
		: PM

Witness Full NAME: 1	Signature:	Phone No:
Address:		Email:
Witness Full NAME: 2	Signature:	Phone No:
Address:		Email:

Notes:

Signer Full NAME:		Phone No:		Record No:	
Address:			Email:		Thumb Print:

Service Performed	Identification	ID Number:	Issued by:	Signature:	
☐ Acknowledgement	☐ ID Card				
☐ Jurat	☐ Driver's License	Issued Date:	Expiration Date:		
☐ Oath	☐ Passport	/ /	/ /		
Other:	☐ Credible Witness	Document Date:	Notary Fee:	Travel Fee:	
	☐ Known Personally	/ /			
	☐				

Document Type:	Date/Time Notarized: / /	: AM
		: PM

Witness Full NAME: 1	Signature:	Phone No:
Address:		Email:
Witness Full NAME: 2	Signature:	Phone No:
Address:		Email:

Notes:

Signer Full NAME:		Phone No:		Record No:

Address: Email: Thumb Print:

Service Performed	Identification	ID Number:	Issued by:	Signature:
☐ Acknowledgement	☐ ID Card			
☐ Jurat	☐ Driver's License	**Issued Date:**	**Expiration Date:**	
☐ Oath	☐ Passport	/ /	/ /	
Other:	☐ Credible Witness	**Document Date:**	**Notary Fee:**	**Travel Fee:**
	☐ Known Personally			
	☐ _____	/ /		

Document Type:	Date/Time Notarized: / /	: AM
		: PM

Witness Full NAME: 1	Signature:	Phone No:
Address:		**Email:**
Witness Full NAME: 2	Signature:	Phone No:
Address:		**Email:**

Notes:

Signer Full NAME:		Phone No:		Record No:

Address: Email: Thumb Print:

Service Performed	Identification	ID Number:	Issued by:	Signature:
☐ Acknowledgement	☐ ID Card			
☐ Jurat	☐ Driver's License	**Issued Date:**	**Expiration Date:**	
☐ Oath	☐ Passport	/ /	/ /	
Other:	☐ Credible Witness	**Document Date:**	**Notary Fee:**	**Travel Fee:**
	☐ Known Personally			
	☐ _____	/ /		

Document Type:	Date/Time Notarized: / /	: AM
		: PM

Witness Full NAME: 1	Signature:	Phone No:
Address:		**Email:**
Witness Full NAME: 2	Signature:	Phone No:
Address:		**Email:**

Notes:

Signer Full NAME:		Phone No:		Record No:	
Address:			Email:		Thumb Print:

Service Performed	Identification	ID Number:	Issued by:	Signature:	
☐ Acknowledgement	☐ ID Card				
☐ Jurat	☐ Driver's License	Issued Date:	Expiration Date:		
☐ Oath	☐ Passport	/ /	/ /		
Other:	☐ Credible Witness	Document Date:	Notary Fee:	Travel Fee:	
	☐ Known Personally	/ /			
	☐ _____				

Document Type:	Date/Time Notarized: / /	: AM
		: PM

Witness Full NAME: 1	Signature:	Phone No:
Address:		Email:
Witness Full NAME: 2	Signature:	Phone No:
Address:		Email:

Notes:

Signer Full NAME:		Phone No:		Record No:	
Address:			Email:		Thumb Print:

Service Performed	Identification	ID Number:	Issued by:	Signature:	
☐ Acknowledgement	☐ ID Card				
☐ Jurat	☐ Driver's License	Issued Date:	Expiration Date:		
☐ Oath	☐ Passport	/ /	/ /		
Other:	☐ Credible Witness	Document Date:	Notary Fee:	Travel Fee:	
	☐ Known Personally	/ /			
	☐ _____				

Document Type:	Date/Time Notarized: / /	: AM
		: PM

Witness Full NAME: 1	Signature:	Phone No:
Address:		Email:
Witness Full NAME: 2	Signature:	Phone No:
Address:		Email:

Notes:

Signer Full NAME:			Phone No:			Record No:

Address:				Email:		Thumb Print:

Service Performed	Identification	ID Number:	Issued by:	Signature:
☐ Acknowledgement ☐ Jurat ☐ Oath Other:	☐ ID Card ☐ Driver's License ☐ Passport ☐ Credible Witness ☐ Known Personally ☐ _____	Issued Date: / /	Expiration Date: / /	
		Document Date: / /	Notary Fee:	Travel Fee:

Document Type:	Date/Time Notarized: / /	: AM : PM

Witness Full NAME: 1	Signature:	Phone No:
Address:		Email:
Witness Full NAME: 2	Signature:	Phone No:
Address:		Email:

Notes:

Signer Full NAME:			Phone No:			Record No:

Address:				Email:		Thumb Print:

Service Performed	Identification	ID Number:	Issued by:	Signature:
☐ Acknowledgement ☐ Jurat ☐ Oath Other:	☐ ID Card ☐ Driver's License ☐ Passport ☐ Credible Witness ☐ Known Personally ☐ _____	Issued Date: / /	Expiration Date: / /	
		Document Date: / /	Notary Fee:	Travel Fee:

Document Type:	Date/Time Notarized: / /	: AM : PM

Witness Full NAME: 1	Signature:	Phone No:
Address:		Email:
Witness Full NAME: 2	Signature:	Phone No:
Address:		Email:

Notes:

Signer Full NAME:		Phone No:		Record No:	
Address:			Email:		Thumb Print:

Service Performed	Identification	ID Number:	Issued by:	Signature:	
☐ Acknowledgement	☐ ID Card				
☐ Jurat	☐ Driver's License	Issued Date:	Expiration Date:		
☐ Oath	☐ Passport	/ /	/ /		
Other:	☐ Credible Witness	Document Date:	Notary Fee:	Travel Fee:	
	☐ Known Personally	/ /			
	☐				

Document Type:	Date/Time Notarized: / /	: AM
		: PM

Witness Full NAME: 1	Signature:	Phone No:
Address:		Email:
Witness Full NAME: 2	Signature:	Phone No:
Address:		Email:

Notes:

Signer Full NAME:		Phone No:		Record No:	
Address:			Email:		Thumb Print:

Service Performed	Identification	ID Number:	Issued by:	Signature:	
☐ Acknowledgement	☐ ID Card				
☐ Jurat	☐ Driver's License	Issued Date:	Expiration Date:		
☐ Oath	☐ Passport	/ /	/ /		
Other:	☐ Credible Witness	Document Date:	Notary Fee:	Travel Fee:	
	☐ Known Personally	/ /			
	☐				

Document Type:	Date/Time Notarized: / /	: AM
		: PM

Witness Full NAME: 1	Signature:	Phone No:
Address:		Email:
Witness Full NAME: 2	Signature:	Phone No:
Address:		Email:

Notes:

Signer Full NAME:		Phone No:		Record No:

Address:		Email:	Thumb Print:

Service Performed	Identification	ID Number:	Issued by:	Signature:
☐ Acknowledgement ☐ Jurat ☐ Oath Other:	☐ ID Card ☐ Driver's License ☐ Passport ☐ Credible Witness ☐ Known Personally ☐ _____	**Issued Date:** / / **Document Date:** / /	**Expiration Date:** / / **Notary Fee:**	**Travel Fee:**

Document Type:	Date/Time Notarized: / /	: AM
		: PM

Witness Full NAME: 1	Signature:	Phone No:
Address:		Email:
Witness Full NAME: 2	Signature:	Phone No:
Address:		Email:

Notes:

Signer Full NAME:		Phone No:		Record No:

Address:		Email:	Thumb Print:

Service Performed	Identification	ID Number:	Issued by:	Signature:
☐ Acknowledgement ☐ Jurat ☐ Oath Other:	☐ ID Card ☐ Driver's License ☐ Passport ☐ Credible Witness ☐ Known Personally ☐ _____	**Issued Date:** / / **Document Date:** / /	**Expiration Date:** / / **Notary Fee:**	**Travel Fee:**

Document Type:	Date/Time Notarized: / /	: AM
		: PM

Witness Full NAME: 1	Signature:	Phone No:
Address:		Email:
Witness Full NAME: 2	Signature:	Phone No:
Address:		Email:

Notes:

Signer Full NAME:		Phone No:		Record No:

Address:		Email:	Thumb Print:

Service Performed	Identification	ID Number:	Issued by:	Signature:
☐ Acknowledgement ☐ Jurat ☐ Oath Other:	☐ ID Card ☐ Driver's License ☐ Passport ☐ Credible Witness ☐ Known Personally ☐ _____	**Issued Date:** / /	**Expiration Date:** / /	
		Document Date: / /	**Notary Fee:**	**Travel Fee:**

Document Type:	Date/Time Notarized: / / : AM : PM

Witness Full NAME: 1	Signature:	Phone No:
Address:		Email:
Witness Full NAME: 2	Signature:	Phone No:
Address:		Email:

Notes:

Signer Full NAME:		Phone No:		Record No:

Address:		Email:	Thumb Print:

Service Performed	Identification	ID Number:	Issued by:	Signature:
☐ Acknowledgement ☐ Jurat ☐ Oath Other:	☐ ID Card ☐ Driver's License ☐ Passport ☐ Credible Witness ☐ Known Personally ☐ _____	**Issued Date:** / /	**Expiration Date:** / /	
		Document Date: / /	**Notary Fee:**	**Travel Fee:**

Document Type:	Date/Time Notarized: / / : AM : PM

Witness Full NAME: 1	Signature:	Phone No:
Address:		Email:
Witness Full NAME: 2	Signature:	Phone No:
Address:		Email:

Notes:

Signer Full NAME:			Phone No:		Record No:	
Address:				Email:		Thumb Print:
Service Performed ☐ Acknowledgement ☐ Jurat ☐ Oath Other:	**Identification** ☐ ID Card ☐ Driver's License ☐ Passport ☐ Credible Witness ☐ Known Personally ☐ _____	ID Number:	Issued by:		Signature:	
		Issued Date: / /	Expiration Date: / /			
		Document Date: / /	Notary Fee:	Travel Fee:		

Document Type:		Date/Time Notarized: / /	: AM : PM
Witness Full NAME: 1	Signature:	Phone No:	
Address:		Email:	
Witness Full NAME: 2	Signature:	Phone No:	
Address:		Email:	

Notes:

Signer Full NAME:			Phone No:		Record No:	
Address:				Email:		Thumb Print:
Service Performed ☐ Acknowledgement ☐ Jurat ☐ Oath Other:	**Identification** ☐ ID Card ☐ Driver's License ☐ Passport ☐ Credible Witness ☐ Known Personally ☐ _____	ID Number:	Issued by:		Signature:	
		Issued Date: / /	Expiration Date: / /			
		Document Date: / /	Notary Fee:	Travel Fee:		

Document Type:		Date/Time Notarized: / /	: AM : PM
Witness Full NAME: 1	Signature:	Phone No:	
Address:		Email:	
Witness Full NAME: 2	Signature:	Phone No:	
Address:		Email:	

Notes:

Signer Full NAME:		Phone No:		Record No:

Address:		Email:		Thumb Print:

Service Performed	Identification	ID Number:	Issued by:	Signature:
□ Acknowledgement □ Jurat □ Oath Other:	□ ID Card □ Driver's License □ Passport □ Credible Witness □ Known Personally □	Issued Date: / /	Expiration Date: / /	
		Document Date: / /	Notary Fee:	Travel Fee:

Document Type:	Date/Time Notarized: / /	: AM : PM

Witness Full NAME: 1	Signature:	Phone No:
Address:		Email:

Witness Full NAME: 2	Signature:	Phone No:
Address:		Email:

Notes:

Signer Full NAME:		Phone No:		Record No:

Address:		Email:		Thumb Print:

Service Performed	Identification	ID Number:	Issued by:	Signature:
□ Acknowledgement □ Jurat □ Oath Other:	□ ID Card □ Driver's License □ Passport □ Credible Witness □ Known Personally □	Issued Date: / /	Expiration Date: / /	
		Document Date: / /	Notary Fee:	Travel Fee:

Document Type:	Date/Time Notarized: / /	: AM : PM

Witness Full NAME: 1	Signature:	Phone No:
Address:		Email:

Witness Full NAME: 2	Signature:	Phone No:
Address:		Email:

Notes:

Signer Full NAME:		Phone No:		Record No:

Address:		Email:	Thumb Print:

Service Performed	Identification	ID Number:	Issued by:	Signature:
☐ Acknowledgement ☐ Jurat ☐ Oath Other:	☐ ID Card ☐ Driver's License ☐ Passport ☐ Credible Witness ☐ Known Personally ☐ _____	**Issued Date:** / / **Document Date:** / /	**Expiration Date:** / / **Notary Fee:**	**Travel Fee:**

Document Type:	Date/Time Notarized: / /	: AM : PM

Witness Full NAME: 1	Signature:	Phone No:
Address:		Email:

Witness Full NAME: 2	Signature:	Phone No:
Address:		Email:

Notes:

Signer Full NAME:		Phone No:		Record No:

Address:		Email:	Thumb Print:

Service Performed	Identification	ID Number:	Issued by:	Signature:
☐ Acknowledgement ☐ Jurat ☐ Oath Other:	☐ ID Card ☐ Driver's License ☐ Passport ☐ Credible Witness ☐ Known Personally ☐ _____	**Issued Date:** / / **Document Date:** / /	**Expiration Date:** / / **Notary Fee:**	**Travel Fee:**

Document Type:	Date/Time Notarized: / /	: AM : PM

Witness Full NAME: 1	Signature:	Phone No:
Address:		Email:

Witness Full NAME: 2	Signature:	Phone No:
Address:		Email:

Notes:

Signer Full NAME:		Phone No:		Record No:	

Address: Email: Thumb Print:

Service Performed	Identification	ID Number:	Issued by:	Signature:
□ Acknowledgement	□ ID Card			
□ Jurat	□ Driver's License	**Issued Date:**	**Expiration Date:**	
□ Oath	□ Passport	/ /	/ /	
Other:	□ Credible Witness	**Document Date:**	**Notary Fee:**	**Travel Fee:**
	□ Known Personally	/ /		
	□ _____			

Document Type:	Date/Time Notarized: / /	: AM
		: PM

Witness Full NAME: 1	Signature:	Phone No:
Address:		Email:
Witness Full NAME: 2	Signature:	Phone No:
Address:		Email:

Notes:

Signer Full NAME:		Phone No:		Record No:	

Address: Email: Thumb Print:

Service Performed	Identification	ID Number:	Issued by:	Signature:
□ Acknowledgement	□ ID Card			
□ Jurat	□ Driver's License	**Issued Date:**	**Expiration Date:**	
□ Oath	□ Passport	/ /	/ /	
Other:	□ Credible Witness	**Document Date:**	**Notary Fee:**	**Travel Fee:**
	□ Known Personally	/ /		
	□ _____			

Document Type:	Date/Time Notarized: / /	: AM
		: PM

Witness Full NAME: 1	Signature:	Phone No:
Address:		Email:
Witness Full NAME: 2	Signature:	Phone No:
Address:		Email:

Notes:

Signer Full NAME:		Phone No:		Record No:	
Address:			Email:		Thumb Print:

Service Performed	Identification	ID Number:	Issued by:	Signature:	
☐ Acknowledgement	☐ ID Card				
☐ Jurat	☐ Driver's License	**Issued Date:**	**Expiration Date:**		
☐ Oath	☐ Passport	/ /	/ /		
Other:	☐ Credible Witness	**Document Date:**	**Notary Fee:**	**Travel Fee:**	
	☐ Known Personally	/ /			
	☐ _____				

Document Type:	Date/Time Notarized: / /	: AM
		: PM

Witness Full NAME: 1	Signature:	Phone No:
Address:		Email:
Witness Full NAME: 2	Signature:	Phone No:
Address:		Email:

Notes:

Signer Full NAME:		Phone No:		Record No:	
Address:			Email:		Thumb Print:

Service Performed	Identification	ID Number:	Issued by:	Signature:	
☐ Acknowledgement	☐ ID Card				
☐ Jurat	☐ Driver's License	**Issued Date:**	**Expiration Date:**		
☐ Oath	☐ Passport	/ /	/ /		
Other:	☐ Credible Witness	**Document Date:**	**Notary Fee:**	**Travel Fee:**	
	☐ Known Personally	/ /			
	☐				

Document Type:	Date/Time Notarized: / /	: AM
		: PM

Witness Full NAME: 1	Signature:	Phone No:
Address:		Email:
Witness Full NAME: 2	Signature:	Phone No:
Address:		Email:

Notes:

Signer Full NAME:		Phone No:		Record No:

Address: **Email:**   **Thumb Print:**

Service Performed	Identification	ID Number:	Issued by:	Signature:
☐ Acknowledgement ☐ Jurat ☐ Oath Other:	☐ ID Card ☐ Driver's License ☐ Passport ☐ Credible Witness ☐ Known Personally ☐ _____	**Issued Date:** / /	**Expiration Date:** / /	
		Document Date: / /	**Notary Fee:**	**Travel Fee:**

Document Type:	Date/Time Notarized: / /	: AM
		: PM

Witness Full NAME: 1	Signature:	Phone No:
Address:		Email:
Witness Full NAME: 2	Signature:	Phone No:
Address:		Email:

Notes:

Signer Full NAME:		Phone No:		Record No:

Address: **Email:**   **Thumb Print:**

Service Performed	Identification	ID Number:	Issued by:	Signature:
☐ Acknowledgement ☐ Jurat ☐ Oath Other:	☐ ID Card ☐ Driver's License ☐ Passport ☐ Credible Witness ☐ Known Personally ☐ _____	**Issued Date:** / /	**Expiration Date:** / /	
		Document Date: / /	**Notary Fee:**	**Travel Fee:**

Document Type:	Date/Time Notarized: / /	: AM
		: PM

Witness Full NAME: 1	Signature:	Phone No:
Address:		Email:
Witness Full NAME: 2	Signature:	Phone No:
Address:		Email:

Notes:

Signer Full NAME:		Phone No:		Record No:

Address: | **Email:** | **Thumb Print:**

Service Performed	Identification	ID Number:	Issued by:	Signature:
☐ Acknowledgement ☐ Jurat ☐ Oath Other:	☐ ID Card ☐ Driver's License ☐ Passport ☐ Credible Witness ☐ Known Personally ☐ _____	**Issued Date:** / / **Document Date:** / /	**Expiration Date:** / / **Notary Fee:**	**Travel Fee:**

Document Type:	Date/Time Notarized: / /	: AM
		: PM

Witness Full NAME: 1	Signature:	Phone No:
Address:		**Email:**
Witness Full NAME: 2	Signature:	Phone No:
Address:		**Email:**

Notes:

Signer Full NAME:		Phone No:		Record No:

Address: | **Email:** | **Thumb Print:**

Service Performed	Identification	ID Number:	Issued by:	Signature:
☐ Acknowledgement ☐ Jurat ☐ Oath Other:	☐ ID Card ☐ Driver's License ☐ Passport ☐ Credible Witness ☐ Known Personally ☐	**Issued Date:** / / **Document Date:** / /	**Expiration Date:** / / **Notary Fee:**	**Travel Fee:**

Document Type:	Date/Time Notarized: / /	: AM
		: PM

Witness Full NAME: 1	Signature:	Phone No:
Address:		**Email:**
Witness Full NAME: 2	Signature:	Phone No:
Address:		**Email:**

Notes:

Signer Full NAME:		Phone No:		Record No:

Address:		Email:	Thumb Print:

Service Performed	Identification	ID Number:	Issued by:	Signature:
☐ Acknowledgement ☐ Jurat ☐ Oath Other:	☐ ID Card ☐ Driver's License ☐ Passport ☐ Credible Witness ☐ Known Personally ☐ _____	Issued Date: / /	Expiration Date: / /	
		Document Date: / /	Notary Fee:	Travel Fee:

Document Type:	Date/Time Notarized: / /	: AM : PM

Witness Full NAME: 1	Signature:	Phone No:
Address:		Email:
Witness Full NAME: 2	Signature:	Phone No:
Address:		Email:

Notes:

Signer Full NAME:		Phone No:		Record No:

Address:		Email:	Thumb Print:

Service Performed	Identification	ID Number:	Issued by:	Signature:
☐ Acknowledgement ☐ Jurat ☐ Oath Other:	☐ ID Card ☐ Driver's License ☐ Passport ☐ Credible Witness ☐ Known Personally ☐ _____	Issued Date: / /	Expiration Date: / /	
		Document Date: / /	Notary Fee:	Travel Fee:

Document Type:	Date/Time Notarized: / /	: AM : PM

Witness Full NAME: 1	Signature:	Phone No:
Address:		Email:
Witness Full NAME: 2	Signature:	Phone No:
Address:		Email:

Notes:

Signer Full NAME:		Phone No:		Record No:	

Address: | **Email:** | **Thumb Print:**

Service Performed	Identification	ID Number:	Issued by:	Signature:
☐ Acknowledgement	☐ ID Card			
☐ Jurat	☐ Driver's License	**Issued Date:**	**Expiration Date:**	
☐ Oath	☐ Passport	/ /	/ /	
Other:	☐ Credible Witness	**Document Date:**	**Notary Fee:**	**Travel Fee:**
	☐ Known Personally	/ /		
	☐ _____			

Document Type:	Date/Time Notarized: / /	: AM
		: PM

Witness Full NAME: 1	Signature:	Phone No:
Address:		Email:
Witness Full NAME: 2	Signature:	Phone No:
Address:		Email:

Notes:

Signer Full NAME:		Phone No:		Record No:	

Address: | **Email:** | **Thumb Print:**

Service Performed	Identification	ID Number:	Issued by:	Signature:
☐ Acknowledgement	☐ ID Card			
☐ Jurat	☐ Driver's License	**Issued Date:**	**Expiration Date:**	
☐ Oath	☐ Passport	/ /	/ /	
Other:	☐ Credible Witness	**Document Date:**	**Notary Fee:**	**Travel Fee:**
	☐ Known Personally	/ /		
	☐ _____			

Document Type:	Date/Time Notarized: / /	: AM
		: PM

Witness Full NAME: 1	Signature:	Phone No:
Address:		Email:
Witness Full NAME: 2	Signature:	Phone No:
Address:		Email:

Notes:

Record 1

Signer Full NAME:		Phone No:		Record No:

Address:	Email:	Thumb Print:

Service Performed	Identification	ID Number:	Issued by:	Signature:
☐ Acknowledgement ☐ Jurat ☐ Oath Other:	☐ ID Card ☐ Driver's License ☐ Passport ☐ Credible Witness ☐ Known Personally ☐ _____	**Issued Date:** / /	**Expiration Date:** / /	
		Document Date: / /	**Notary Fee:**	**Travel Fee:**

Document Type:	Date/Time Notarized: / /	: AM : PM

Witness Full NAME: 1	Signature:	Phone No:
Address:		Email:
Witness Full NAME: 2	Signature:	Phone No:
Address:		Email:

Notes:

Record 2

Signer Full NAME:		Phone No:		Record No:

Address:	Email:	Thumb Print:

Service Performed	Identification	ID Number:	Issued by:	Signature:
☐ Acknowledgement ☐ Jurat ☐ Oath Other:	☐ ID Card ☐ Driver's License ☐ Passport ☐ Credible Witness ☐ Known Personally ☐ _____	**Issued Date:** / /	**Expiration Date:** / /	
		Document Date: / /	**Notary Fee:**	**Travel Fee:**

Document Type:	Date/Time Notarized: / /	: AM : PM

Witness Full NAME: 1	Signature:	Phone No:
Address:		Email:
Witness Full NAME: 2	Signature:	Phone No:
Address:		Email:

Notes:

Signer Full NAME:		Phone No:		Record No:
Address:		Email:		Thumb Print:

Service Performed	Identification	ID Number:	Issued by:	Signature:
☐ Acknowledgement ☐ Jurat ☐ Oath Other:	☐ ID Card ☐ Driver's License ☐ Passport ☐ Credible Witness ☐ Known Personally ☐ _____	**Issued Date:** / / **Document Date:** / /	**Expiration Date:** / / **Notary Fee:**	**Travel Fee:**

Document Type:	Date/Time Notarized: / /	: AM : PM

Witness Full NAME: 1	Signature:	Phone No:
Address:		Email:

Witness Full NAME: 2	Signature:	Phone No:
Address:		Email:

Notes:

Signer Full NAME:		Phone No:		Record No:
Address:		Email:		Thumb Print:

Service Performed	Identification	ID Number:	Issued by:	Signature:
☐ Acknowledgement ☐ Jurat ☐ Oath Other:	☐ ID Card ☐ Driver's License ☐ Passport ☐ Credible Witness ☐ Known Personally ☐ _____	**Issued Date:** / / **Document Date:** / /	**Expiration Date:** / / **Notary Fee:**	**Travel Fee:**

Document Type:	Date/Time Notarized: / /	: AM : PM

Witness Full NAME: 1	Signature:	Phone No:
Address:		Email:

Witness Full NAME: 2	Signature:	Phone No:
Address:		Email:

Notes:

Signer Full NAME: | **Phone No:** | **Record No:**

Address: | **Email:** | **Thumb Print:**

Service Performed	Identification	ID Number:	Issued by:	Signature:
☐ Acknowledgement ☐ Jurat ☐ Oath Other:	☐ ID Card ☐ Driver's License ☐ Passport ☐ Credible Witness ☐ Known Personally ☐ _____	**Issued Date:** / /	**Expiration Date:** / /	
		Document Date: / /	**Notary Fee:**	**Travel Fee:**

Document Type: | **Date/Time Notarized:** / / | : AM
: PM

Witness Full NAME: 1 | **Signature:** | **Phone No:**

Address: | | **Email:**

Witness Full NAME: 2 | **Signature:** | **Phone No:**

Address: | | **Email:**

Notes:

Signer Full NAME: | **Phone No:** | **Record No:**

Address: | **Email:** | **Thumb Print:**

Service Performed	Identification	ID Number:	Issued by:	Signature:
☐ Acknowledgement ☐ Jurat ☐ Oath Other:	☐ ID Card ☐ Driver's License ☐ Passport ☐ Credible Witness ☐ Known Personally ☐ _____	**Issued Date:** / /	**Expiration Date:** / /	
		Document Date: / /	**Notary Fee:**	**Travel Fee:**

Document Type: | **Date/Time Notarized:** / / | : AM
: PM

Witness Full NAME: 1 | **Signature:** | **Phone No:**

Address: | | **Email:**

Witness Full NAME: 2 | **Signature:** | **Phone No:**

Address: | | **Email:**

Notes:

Signer Full NAME:	Phone No:	Record No:

Address:	Email:	Thumb Print:

Service Performed	Identification	ID Number:	Issued by:	Signature:
☐ Acknowledgement	☐ ID Card			
☐ Jurat	☐ Driver's License	**Issued Date:**	**Expiration Date:**	
☐ Oath	☐ Passport	/ /	/ /	
Other:	☐ Credible Witness	**Document Date:**	**Notary Fee:**	**Travel Fee:**
	☐ Known Personally	/ /		
	☐ _____			

Document Type:	Date/Time Notarized: / /	:	AM
		:	PM

Witness Full NAME: 1	Signature:	Phone No:
Address:		Email:
Witness Full NAME: 2	Signature:	Phone No:
Address:		Email:

Notes:

Signer Full NAME:	Phone No:	Record No:

Address:	Email:	Thumb Print:

Service Performed	Identification	ID Number:	Issued by:	Signature:
☐ Acknowledgement	☐ ID Card			
☐ Jurat	☐ Driver's License	**Issued Date:**	**Expiration Date:**	
☐ Oath	☐ Passport	/ /	/ /	
Other:	☐ Credible Witness	**Document Date:**	**Notary Fee:**	**Travel Fee:**
	☐ Known Personally	/ /		
	☐ _____			

Document Type:	Date/Time Notarized: / /	:	AM
		:	PM

Witness Full NAME: 1	Signature:	Phone No:
Address:		Email:
Witness Full NAME: 2	Signature:	Phone No:
Address:		Email:

Notes:

Signer Full NAME:		Phone No:		Record No:	
Address:			Email:		Thumb Print:

Service Performed	Identification	ID Number:	Issued by:	Signature:	
☐ Acknowledgement ☐ Jurat ☐ Oath Other:	☐ ID Card ☐ Driver's License ☐ Passport ☐ Credible Witness ☐ Known Personally ☐ _____	Issued Date: / /	Expiration Date: / /		
		Document Date: / /	Notary Fee:	Travel Fee:	

Document Type:	Date/Time Notarized: / /	: AM
		: PM

Witness Full NAME: 1	Signature:	Phone No:
Address:		Email:

Witness Full NAME: 2	Signature:	Phone No:
Address:		Email:

Notes:

Signer Full NAME:		Phone No:		Record No:	
Address:			Email:		Thumb Print:

Service Performed	Identification	ID Number:	Issued by:	Signature:	
☐ Acknowledgement ☐ Jurat ☐ Oath Other:	☐ ID Card ☐ Driver's License ☐ Passport ☐ Credible Witness ☐ Known Personally ☐ _____	Issued Date: / /	Expiration Date: / /		
		Document Date: / /	Notary Fee:	Travel Fee:	

Document Type:	Date/Time Notarized: / /	: AM
		: PM

Witness Full NAME: 1	Signature:	Phone No:
Address:		Email:

Witness Full NAME: 2	Signature:	Phone No:
Address:		Email:

Notes:

Signer Full NAME:		Phone No:		Record No:	

Address: | **Email:** | **Thumb Print:**

Service Performed	Identification	ID Number:	Issued by:	Signature:	
☐ Acknowledgement	☐ ID Card				
☐ Jurat	☐ Driver's License	**Issued Date:**	**Expiration Date:**		
☐ Oath	☐ Passport	/ /	/ /		
Other:	☐ Credible Witness	**Document Date:**	**Notary Fee:**	**Travel Fee:**	
	☐ Known Personally	/ /			
	☐ _____				

Document Type:	Date/Time Notarized: / /	: AM
		: PM

Witness Full NAME: 1	Signature:	Phone No:
Address:		Email:
Witness Full NAME: 2	Signature:	Phone No:
Address:		Email:

Notes:

Signer Full NAME:		Phone No:		Record No:	

Address: | **Email:** | **Thumb Print:**

Service Performed	Identification	ID Number:	Issued by:	Signature:	
☐ Acknowledgement	☐ ID Card				
☐ Jurat	☐ Driver's License	**Issued Date:**	**Expiration Date:**		
☐ Oath	☐ Passport	/ /	/ /		
Other:	☐ Credible Witness	**Document Date:**	**Notary Fee:**	**Travel Fee:**	
	☐ Known Personally	/ /			
	☐				

Document Type:	Date/Time Notarized: / /	: AM
		: PM

Witness Full NAME: 1	Signature:	Phone No:
Address:		Email:
Witness Full NAME: 2	Signature:	Phone No:
Address:		Email:

Notes:

Signer Full NAME:		Phone No:		Record No:
Address:			Email:	Thumb Print:

Service Performed	Identification	ID Number:	Issued by:	Signature:
□ Acknowledgement □ Jurat □ Oath Other:	□ ID Card □ Driver's License □ Passport □ Credible Witness □ Known Personally □ _____	Issued Date: / /	Expiration Date: / /	
		Document Date: / /	Notary Fee:	Travel Fee:

Document Type:	Date/Time Notarized: / /	: AM : PM

Witness Full NAME: 1	Signature:	Phone No:
Address:		Email:
Witness Full NAME: 2	Signature:	Phone No:
Address:		Email:

Notes:

Signer Full NAME:		Phone No:		Record No:
Address:			Email:	Thumb Print:

Service Performed	Identification	ID Number:	Issued by:	Signature:
□ Acknowledgement □ Jurat □ Oath Other:	□ ID Card □ Driver's License □ Passport □ Credible Witness □ Known Personally □ _____	Issued Date: / /	Expiration Date: / /	
		Document Date: / /	Notary Fee:	Travel Fee:

Document Type:	Date/Time Notarized: / /	: AM : PM

Witness Full NAME: 1	Signature:	Phone No:
Address:		Email:
Witness Full NAME: 2	Signature:	Phone No:
Address:		Email:

Notes:

Signer Full NAME:			Phone No:		Record No:	
Address:				Email:		Thumb Print:

Service Performed	Identification	ID Number:	Issued by:	Signature:	
☐ Acknowledgement ☐ Jurat ☐ Oath Other:	☐ ID Card ☐ Driver's License ☐ Passport ☐ Credible Witness ☐ Known Personally ☐ _____	Issued Date: / /	Expiration Date: / /		
		Document Date: / /	Notary Fee:	Travel Fee:	

Document Type:		Date/Time Notarized: / /	: AM : PM

Witness Full NAME: 1	Signature:	Phone No:
Address:		Email:
Witness Full NAME: 2	Signature:	Phone No:
Address:		Email:

Notes:

Signer Full NAME:			Phone No:		Record No:	
Address:				Email:		Thumb Print:

Service Performed	Identification	ID Number:	Issued by:	Signature:	
☐ Acknowledgement ☐ Jurat ☐ Oath Other:	☐ ID Card ☐ Driver's License ☐ Passport ☐ Credible Witness ☐ Known Personally ☐ _____	Issued Date: / /	Expiration Date: / /		
		Document Date: / /	Notary Fee:	Travel Fee:	

Document Type:		Date/Time Notarized: / /	: AM : PM

Witness Full NAME: 1	Signature:	Phone No:
Address:		Email:
Witness Full NAME: 2	Signature:	Phone No:
Address:		Email:

Notes:

Signer Full NAME:		Phone No:		Record No:

Address:		Email:	Thumb Print:

Service Performed	Identification	ID Number:	Issued by:	Signature:
☐ Acknowledgement ☐ Jurat ☐ Oath Other:	☐ ID Card ☐ Driver's License ☐ Passport ☐ Credible Witness ☐ Known Personally ☐ _____	**Issued Date:** / /	**Expiration Date:** / /	
		Document Date: / /	**Notary Fee:**	**Travel Fee:**

Document Type:	Date/Time Notarized: / /	: AM : PM

Witness Full NAME: 1	Signature:	Phone No:
Address:		Email:

Witness Full NAME: 2	Signature:	Phone No:
Address:		Email:

Notes:

Signer Full NAME:		Phone No:		Record No:

Address:		Email:	Thumb Print:

Service Performed	Identification	ID Number:	Issued by:	Signature:
☐ Acknowledgement ☐ Jurat ☐ Oath Other:	☐ ID Card ☐ Driver's License ☐ Passport ☐ Credible Witness ☐ Known Personally ☐ _____	**Issued Date:** / /	**Expiration Date:** / /	
		Document Date: / /	**Notary Fee:**	**Travel Fee:**

Document Type:	Date/Time Notarized: / /	: AM : PM

Witness Full NAME: 1	Signature:	Phone No:
Address:		Email:

Witness Full NAME: 2	Signature:	Phone No:
Address:		Email:

Notes:

Signer Full NAME:	Phone No:	Record No:

Address:	Email:	Thumb Print:

Service Performed	Identification	ID Number:	Issued by:	Signature:
□ Acknowledgement □ Jurat □ Oath Other:	□ ID Card □ Driver's License □ Passport □ Credible Witness □ Known Personally □ _____	Issued Date: / / Document Date: / /	Expiration Date: / / Notary Fee:	 Travel Fee:

Document Type:	Date/Time Notarized: / /	: AM : PM

Witness Full NAME: 1	Signature:	Phone No:
Address:		Email:
Witness Full NAME: 2	Signature:	Phone No:
Address:		Email:

Notes:

Signer Full NAME:	Phone No:	Record No:

Address:	Email:	Thumb Print:

Service Performed	Identification	ID Number:	Issued by:	Signature:
□ Acknowledgement □ Jurat □ Oath Other:	□ ID Card □ Driver's License □ Passport □ Credible Witness □ Known Personally □ _____	Issued Date: / / Document Date: / /	Expiration Date: / / Notary Fee:	 Travel Fee:

Document Type:	Date/Time Notarized: / /	: AM : PM

Witness Full NAME: 1	Signature:	Phone No:
Address:		Email:
Witness Full NAME: 2	Signature:	Phone No:
Address:		Email:

Notes:

Signer Full NAME:		Phone No:		Record No:

Address: **Email:**   **Thumb Print:**

Service Performed	Identification	ID Number:	Issued by:	Signature:
☐ Acknowledgement	☐ ID Card			
☐ Jurat	☐ Driver's License	**Issued Date:** / /	**Expiration Date:** / /	
☐ Oath	☐ Passport			
Other:	☐ Credible Witness	**Document Date:** / /	**Notary Fee:**	**Travel Fee:**
	☐ Known Personally ☐			

Document Type:	Date/Time Notarized: / /	: AM
		: PM

Witness Full NAME: 1	Signature:	Phone No:
Address:		Email:
Witness Full NAME: 2	Signature:	Phone No:
Address:		Email:

Notes:

Signer Full NAME:		Phone No:		Record No:

Address: **Email:**   **Thumb Print:**

Service Performed	Identification	ID Number:	Issued by:	Signature:
☐ Acknowledgement	☐ ID Card			
☐ Jurat	☐ Driver's License	**Issued Date:** / /	**Expiration Date:** / /	
☐ Oath	☐ Passport			
Other:	☐ Credible Witness	**Document Date:** / /	**Notary Fee:**	**Travel Fee:**
	☐ Known Personally ☐			

Document Type:	Date/Time Notarized: / /	: AM
		: PM

Witness Full NAME: 1	Signature:	Phone No:
Address:		Email:
Witness Full NAME: 2	Signature:	Phone No:
Address:		Email:

Notes:

Signer Full NAME:		Phone No:		Record No:	

Address: **Email:**   **Thumb Print:**

Service Performed	Identification	ID Number:	Issued by:	Signature:
☐ Acknowledgement ☐ Jurat ☐ Oath Other:	☐ ID Card ☐ Driver's License ☐ Passport ☐ Credible Witness ☐ Known Personally ☐ _____	**Issued Date:** / /	**Expiration Date:** / /	
		Document Date: / /	**Notary Fee:**	**Travel Fee:**

Document Type:	Date/Time Notarized: / /	: AM : PM

Witness Full NAME: 1	Signature:	Phone No:
Address:		Email:
Witness Full NAME: 2	Signature:	Phone No:
Address:		Email:

Notes:

Signer Full NAME:		Phone No:		Record No:	

Address: **Email:**   **Thumb Print:**

Service Performed	Identification	ID Number:	Issued by:	Signature:
☐ Acknowledgement ☐ Jurat ☐ Oath Other:	☐ ID Card ☐ Driver's License ☐ Passport ☐ Credible Witness ☐ Known Personally ☐ _____	**Issued Date:** / /	**Expiration Date:** / /	
		Document Date: / /	**Notary Fee:**	**Travel Fee:**

Document Type:	Date/Time Notarized: / /	: AM : PM

Witness Full NAME: 1	Signature:	Phone No:
Address:		Email:
Witness Full NAME: 2	Signature:	Phone No:
Address:		Email:

Notes:

Signer Full NAME:		Phone No:		Record No:

Address:		Email:	Thumb Print:

Service Performed	Identification	ID Number:	Issued by:	Signature:
☐ Acknowledgement	☐ ID Card			
☐ Jurat	☐ Driver's License	**Issued Date:**	**Expiration Date:**	
☐ Oath	☐ Passport	/ /	/ /	
Other:	☐ Credible Witness	**Document Date:**	**Notary Fee:**	**Travel Fee:**
	☐ Known Personally	/ /		
	☐ _____			

Document Type:	Date/Time Notarized: / /	: AM
		: PM

Witness Full NAME: 1	Signature:	Phone No:
Address:		Email:

Witness Full NAME: 2	Signature:	Phone No:
Address:		Email:

Notes:

Signer Full NAME:		Phone No:		Record No:

Address:		Email:	Thumb Print:

Service Performed	Identification	ID Number:	Issued by:	Signature:
☐ Acknowledgement	☐ ID Card			
☐ Jurat	☐ Driver's License	**Issued Date:**	**Expiration Date:**	
☐ Oath	☐ Passport	/ /	/ /	
Other:	☐ Credible Witness	**Document Date:**	**Notary Fee:**	**Travel Fee:**
	☐ Known Personally	/ /		
	☐			

Document Type:	Date/Time Notarized: / /	: AM
		: PM

Witness Full NAME: 1	Signature:	Phone No:
Address:		Email:

Witness Full NAME: 2	Signature:	Phone No:
Address:		Email:

Notes:

Signer Full NAME:		Phone No:		Record No:

Address:		Email:	Thumb Print:

Service Performed	Identification	ID Number:	Issued by:	Signature:
☐ Acknowledgement ☐ Jurat ☐ Oath Other:	☐ ID Card ☐ Driver's License ☐ Passport ☐ Credible Witness ☐ Known Personally ☐ _____	**Issued Date:** / /	**Expiration Date:** / /	
		Document Date: / /	**Notary Fee:**	**Travel Fee:**

Document Type:	Date/Time Notarized: / /	: AM : PM

Witness Full NAME: 1	Signature:	Phone No:
Address:		Email:

Witness Full NAME: 2	Signature:	Phone No:
Address:		Email:

Notes:

Signer Full NAME:		Phone No:		Record No:

Address:		Email:	Thumb Print:

Service Performed	Identification	ID Number:	Issued by:	Signature:
☐ Acknowledgement ☐ Jurat ☐ Oath Other:	☐ ID Card ☐ Driver's License ☐ Passport ☐ Credible Witness ☐ Known Personally ☐ _____	**Issued Date:** / /	**Expiration Date:** / /	
		Document Date: / /	**Notary Fee:**	**Travel Fee:**

Document Type:	Date/Time Notarized: / /	: AM : PM

Witness Full NAME: 1	Signature:	Phone No:
Address:		Email:

Witness Full NAME: 2	Signature:	Phone No:
Address:		Email:

Notes:

Signer Full NAME:		Phone No:		Record No:	
Address:			Email:		Thumb Print:

Service Performed	Identification	ID Number:	Issued by:	Signature:	
□ Acknowledgement	□ ID Card				
□ Jurat	□ Driver's License	Issued Date:	Expiration Date:		
□ Oath	□ Passport	/ /	/ /		
Other:	□ Credible Witness	Document Date:	Notary Fee:	Travel Fee:	
	□ Known Personally	/ /			
	□ _____				

Document Type:	Date/Time Notarized: / /	: AM
		: PM

Witness Full NAME: 1	Signature:	Phone No:
Address:		Email:
Witness Full NAME: 2	Signature:	Phone No:
Address:		Email:

Notes:

Signer Full NAME:		Phone No:		Record No:	
Address:			Email:		Thumb Print:

Service Performed	Identification	ID Number:	Issued by:	Signature:	
□ Acknowledgement	□ ID Card				
□ Jurat	□ Driver's License	Issued Date:	Expiration Date:		
□ Oath	□ Passport	/ /	/ /		
Other:	□ Credible Witness	Document Date:	Notary Fee:	Travel Fee:	
	□ Known Personally	/ /			
	□ _____				

Document Type:	Date/Time Notarized: / /	: AM
		: PM

Witness Full NAME: 1	Signature:	Phone No:
Address:		Email:
Witness Full NAME: 2	Signature:	Phone No:
Address:		Email:

Notes:

Signer Full NAME:		Phone No:		Record No:	
Address:			Email:		Thumb Print:

Service Performed	Identification	ID Number:	Issued by:	Signature:	
☐ Acknowledgement	☐ ID Card				
☐ Jurat	☐ Driver's License	Issued Date:	Expiration Date:		
☐ Oath	☐ Passport	/ /	/ /		
Other:	☐ Credible Witness	Document Date:	Notary Fee:	Travel Fee:	
	☐ Known Personally				
	☐ _____	/ /			

Document Type:		Date/Time Notarized: / /	: AM
			: PM

Witness Full NAME: 1	Signature:	Phone No:
Address:		Email:
Witness Full NAME: 2	Signature:	Phone No:
Address:		Email:

Notes:

Signer Full NAME:		Phone No:		Record No:	
Address:			Email:		Thumb Print:

Service Performed	Identification	ID Number:	Issued by:	Signature:	
☐ Acknowledgement	☐ ID Card				
☐ Jurat	☐ Driver's License	Issued Date:	Expiration Date:		
☐ Oath	☐ Passport	/ /	/ /		
Other:	☐ Credible Witness	Document Date:	Notary Fee:	Travel Fee:	
	☐ Known Personally				
	☐ _____	/ /			

Document Type:		Date/Time Notarized: / /	: AM
			: PM

Witness Full NAME: 1	Signature:	Phone No:
Address:		Email:
Witness Full NAME: 2	Signature:	Phone No:
Address:		Email:

Notes:

Signer Full NAME:		Phone No:		Record No:

Address:		Email:	Thumb Print:

Service Performed	Identification	ID Number:	Issued by:	Signature:
□ Acknowledgement	□ ID Card			
□ Jurat	□ Driver's License	Issued Date:	Expiration Date:	
□ Oath	□ Passport	/ /	/ /	
Other:	□ Credible Witness	Document Date:	Notary Fee:	Travel Fee:
	□ Known Personally			
	□ _____	/ /		

Document Type:		Date/Time Notarized: / /	: AM
			: PM

Witness Full NAME: 1	Signature:	Phone No:
Address:		Email:

Witness Full NAME: 2	Signature:	Phone No:
Address:		Email:

Notes:

Signer Full NAME:		Phone No:		Record No:

Address:		Email:	Thumb Print:

Service Performed	Identification	ID Number:	Issued by:	Signature:
□ Acknowledgement	□ ID Card			
□ Jurat	□ Driver's License	Issued Date:	Expiration Date:	
□ Oath	□ Passport	/ /	/ /	
Other:	□ Credible Witness	Document Date:	Notary Fee:	Travel Fee:
	□ Known Personally			
	□ _____	/ /		

Document Type:		Date/Time Notarized: / /	: AM
			: PM

Witness Full NAME: 1	Signature:	Phone No:
Address:		Email:

Witness Full NAME: 2	Signature:	Phone No:
Address:		Email:

Notes:

Signer Full NAME:		Phone No:		Record No:

Address: | **Email:** | **Thumb Print:**

Service Performed	Identification	ID Number:	Issued by:	Signature:
☐ Acknowledgement	☐ ID Card			
☐ Jurat	☐ Driver's License	**Issued Date:**	**Expiration Date:**	
☐ Oath	☐ Passport	/ /	/ /	
Other:	☐ Credible Witness	**Document Date:**	**Notary Fee:**	**Travel Fee:**
	☐ Known Personally			
	☐ _____	/ /		

Document Type:	Date/Time Notarized: / /	: AM
		: PM

Witness Full NAME: 1	Signature:	Phone No:
Address:		Email:
Witness Full NAME: 2	Signature:	Phone No:
Address:		Email:

Notes:

Signer Full NAME:		Phone No:		Record No:

Address: | **Email:** | **Thumb Print:**

Service Performed	Identification	ID Number:	Issued by:	Signature:
☐ Acknowledgement	☐ ID Card			
☐ Jurat	☐ Driver's License	**Issued Date:**	**Expiration Date:**	
☐ Oath	☐ Passport	/ /	/ /	
Other:	☐ Credible Witness	**Document Date:**	**Notary Fee:**	**Travel Fee:**
	☐ Known Personally			
	☐ _____	/ /		

Document Type:	Date/Time Notarized: / /	: AM
		: PM

Witness Full NAME: 1	Signature:	Phone No:
Address:		Email:
Witness Full NAME: 2	Signature:	Phone No:
Address:		Email:

Notes:

Signer Full NAME:		Phone No:		Record No:

Address:	Email:	Thumb Print:

Service Performed	Identification	ID Number:	Issued by:	Signature:
☐ Acknowledgement	☐ ID Card			
☐ Jurat	☐ Driver's License	**Issued Date:**	**Expiration Date:**	
☐ Oath	☐ Passport	/ /	/ /	
Other:	☐ Credible Witness	**Document Date:**	**Notary Fee:**	**Travel Fee:**
	☐ Known Personally			
	☐	/ /		

Document Type:	Date/Time Notarized: / /	: AM
		: PM

Witness Full NAME: 1	Signature:	Phone No:
Address:		Email:
Witness Full NAME: 2	Signature:	Phone No:
Address:		Email:

Notes:

Signer Full NAME:		Phone No:		Record No:

Address:	Email:	Thumb Print:

Service Performed	Identification	ID Number:	Issued by:	Signature:
☐ Acknowledgement	☐ ID Card			
☐ Jurat	☐ Driver's License	**Issued Date:**	**Expiration Date:**	
☐ Oath	☐ Passport	/ /	/ /	
Other:	☐ Credible Witness	**Document Date:**	**Notary Fee:**	**Travel Fee:**
	☐ Known Personally			
	☐	/ /		

Document Type:	Date/Time Notarized: / /	: AM
		: PM

Witness Full NAME: 1	Signature:	Phone No:
Address:		Email:
Witness Full NAME: 2	Signature:	Phone No:
Address:		Email:

Notes:

Signer Full NAME:		Phone No:		Record No:

Address:		Email:		Thumb Print:

Service Performed	Identification	ID Number:	Issued by:	Signature:
□ Acknowledgement	□ ID Card			
□ Jurat	□ Driver's License	**Issued Date:**	**Expiration Date:**	
□ Oath	□ Passport	/ /	/ /	
Other:	□ Credible Witness	**Document Date:**	**Notary Fee:**	**Travel Fee:**
	□ Known Personally			
	□ _____	/ /		

Document Type:	Date/Time Notarized: / /	: AM
		: PM

Witness Full NAME: 1	Signature:	Phone No:
Address:		Email:
Witness Full NAME: 2	Signature:	Phone No:
Address:		Email:

Notes:

Signer Full NAME:		Phone No:		Record No:

Address:		Email:		Thumb Print:

Service Performed	Identification	ID Number:	Issued by:	Signature:
□ Acknowledgement	□ ID Card			
□ Jurat	□ Driver's License	**Issued Date:**	**Expiration Date:**	
□ Oath	□ Passport	/ /	/ /	
Other:	□ Credible Witness	**Document Date:**	**Notary Fee:**	**Travel Fee:**
	□ Known Personally			
	□ _____	/ /		

Document Type:	Date/Time Notarized: / /	: AM
		: PM

Witness Full NAME: 1	Signature:	Phone No:
Address:		Email:
Witness Full NAME: 2	Signature:	Phone No:
Address:		Email:

Notes:

Signer Full NAME:	Phone No:	Record No:

Address:	Email:	Thumb Print:

Service Performed	Identification	ID Number:	Issued by:	Signature:
☐ Acknowledgement	☐ ID Card			
☐ Jurat	☐ Driver's License	**Issued Date:**	**Expiration Date:**	
☐ Oath	☐ Passport	/ /	/ /	
Other:	☐ Credible Witness	**Document Date:**	**Notary Fee:**	**Travel Fee:**
	☐ Known Personally	/ /		
	☐ _____			

Document Type:	Date/Time Notarized: / /	: AM
		: PM

Witness Full NAME: 1	Signature:	Phone No:
Address:		Email:
Witness Full NAME: 2	Signature:	Phone No:
Address:		Email:

Notes:

Signer Full NAME:	Phone No:	Record No:

Address:	Email:	Thumb Print:

Service Performed	Identification	ID Number:	Issued by:	Signature:
☐ Acknowledgement	☐ ID Card			
☐ Jurat	☐ Driver's License	**Issued Date:**	**Expiration Date:**	
☐ Oath	☐ Passport	/ /	/ /	
Other:	☐ Credible Witness	**Document Date:**	**Notary Fee:**	**Travel Fee:**
	☐ Known Personally	/ /		
	☐ _____			

Document Type:	Date/Time Notarized: / /	: AM
		: PM

Witness Full NAME: 1	Signature:	Phone No:
Address:		Email:
Witness Full NAME: 2	Signature:	Phone No:
Address:		Email:

Notes:

Signer Full NAME:		Phone No:		Record No:	
Address:			**Email:**		**Thumb Print:**

Service Performed	**Identification**	**ID Number:**	**Issued by:**	**Signature:**
☐ Acknowledgement ☐ Jurat ☐ Oath Other:	☐ ID Card ☐ Driver's License ☐ Passport ☐ Credible Witness ☐ Known Personally ☐ _____	**Issued Date:** / /	**Expiration Date:** / /	
		Document Date: / /	**Notary Fee:**	**Travel Fee:**

Document Type:	**Date/Time Notarized:** / / : AM : PM

Witness Full NAME: 1	**Signature:**	**Phone No:**
Address:		**Email:**
Witness Full NAME: 2	**Signature:**	**Phone No:**
Address:		**Email:**

Notes:

Signer Full NAME:		Phone No:		Record No:	
Address:			**Email:**		**Thumb Print:**

Service Performed	**Identification**	**ID Number:**	**Issued by:**	**Signature:**
☐ Acknowledgement ☐ Jurat ☐ Oath Other:	☐ ID Card ☐ Driver's License ☐ Passport ☐ Credible Witness ☐ Known Personally ☐ _____	**Issued Date:** / /	**Expiration Date:** / /	
		Document Date: / /	**Notary Fee:**	**Travel Fee:**

Document Type:	**Date/Time Notarized:** / / : AM : PM

Witness Full NAME: 1	**Signature:**	**Phone No:**
Address:		**Email:**
Witness Full NAME: 2	**Signature:**	**Phone No:**
Address:		**Email:**

Notes:

Signer Full NAME:		Phone No:		Record No:
Address:			Email:	Thumb Print:

Service Performed	Identification	ID Number:	Issued by:	Signature:
☐ Acknowledgement ☐ Jurat ☐ Oath Other:	☐ ID Card ☐ Driver's License ☐ Passport ☐ Credible Witness ☐ Known Personally ☐ _____	**Issued Date:** / / **Document Date:** / /	**Expiration Date:** / / **Notary Fee:**	**Travel Fee:**

Document Type:	Date/Time Notarized: / /	: AM
		: PM

Witness Full NAME: 1	Signature:	Phone No:
Address:		Email:
Witness Full NAME: 2	Signature:	Phone No:
Address:		Email:

Notes:

Signer Full NAME:		Phone No:		Record No:
Address:			Email:	Thumb Print:

Service Performed	Identification	ID Number:	Issued by:	Signature:
☐ Acknowledgement ☐ Jurat ☐ Oath Other:	☐ ID Card ☐ Driver's License ☐ Passport ☐ Credible Witness ☐ Known Personally ☐ _____	**Issued Date:** / / **Document Date:** / /	**Expiration Date:** / / **Notary Fee:**	**Travel Fee:**

Document Type:	Date/Time Notarized: / /	: AM
		: PM

Witness Full NAME: 1	Signature:	Phone No:
Address:		Email:
Witness Full NAME: 2	Signature:	Phone No:
Address:		Email:

Notes:

Signer Full NAME:		Phone No:		Record No:	
Address:			Email:		Thumb Print:

Service Performed	Identification	ID Number:	Issued by:	Signature:	
☐ Acknowledgement ☐ Jurat ☐ Oath Other:	☐ ID Card ☐ Driver's License ☐ Passport ☐ Credible Witness ☐ Known Personally ☐ _____	**Issued Date:** / /	**Expiration Date:** / /		
		Document Date: / /	**Notary Fee:**	**Travel Fee:**	

Document Type:	Date/Time Notarized: / /	: AM : PM

Witness Full NAME: 1	Signature:	Phone No:
Address:		Email:
Witness Full NAME: 2	Signature:	Phone No:
Address:		Email:

Notes:

Signer Full NAME:		Phone No:		Record No:	
Address:			Email:		Thumb Print:

Service Performed	Identification	ID Number:	Issued by:	Signature:	
☐ Acknowledgement ☐ Jurat ☐ Oath Other:	☐ ID Card ☐ Driver's License ☐ Passport ☐ Credible Witness ☐ Known Personally ☐ _____	**Issued Date:** / /	**Expiration Date:** / /		
		Document Date: / /	**Notary Fee:**	**Travel Fee:**	

Document Type:	Date/Time Notarized: / /	: AM : PM

Witness Full NAME: 1	Signature:	Phone No:
Address:		Email:
Witness Full NAME: 2	Signature:	Phone No:
Address:		Email:

Notes:

Signer Full NAME:		Phone No:		Record No:	
Address:			Email:		Thumb Print:

Service Performed	Identification	ID Number:	Issued by:	Signature:	
☐ Acknowledgement ☐ Jurat ☐ Oath Other:	☐ ID Card ☐ Driver's License ☐ Passport ☐ Credible Witness ☐ Known Personally ☐ _____	Issued Date: / /	Expiration Date: / /		
		Document Date: / /	Notary Fee:	Travel Fee:	

Document Type:		Date/Time Notarized: / /	: AM : PM
Witness Full NAME: 1	Signature:	Phone No:	
Address:		Email:	
Witness Full NAME: 2	Signature:	Phone No:	
Address:		Email:	

Notes:

Signer Full NAME:		Phone No:		Record No:	
Address:			Email:		Thumb Print:

Service Performed	Identification	ID Number:	Issued by:	Signature:	
☐ Acknowledgement ☐ Jurat ☐ Oath Other:	☐ ID Card ☐ Driver's License ☐ Passport ☐ Credible Witness ☐ Known Personally ☐ _____	Issued Date: / /	Expiration Date: / /		
		Document Date: / /	Notary Fee:	Travel Fee:	

Document Type:		Date/Time Notarized: / /	: AM : PM
Witness Full NAME: 1	Signature:	Phone No:	
Address:		Email:	
Witness Full NAME: 2	Signature:	Phone No:	
Address:		Email:	

Notes:

Signer Full NAME:		Phone No:		Record No:	

Address: | **Email:** | **Thumb Print:**

Service Performed	Identification	ID Number:	Issued by:	Signature:
☐ Acknowledgement	☐ ID Card			
☐ Jurat	☐ Driver's License	**Issued Date:**	**Expiration Date:**	
☐ Oath	☐ Passport	/ /	/ /	
Other:	☐ Credible Witness	**Document Date:**	**Notary Fee:**	**Travel Fee:**
	☐ Known Personally			
	☐ _____	/ /		

Document Type:	Date/Time Notarized: / /	: AM
		: PM

Witness Full NAME: 1	Signature:	Phone No:
Address:		**Email:**
Witness Full NAME: 2	Signature:	Phone No:
Address:		**Email:**

Notes:

Signer Full NAME:		Phone No:		Record No:	

Address: | **Email:** | **Thumb Print:**

Service Performed	Identification	ID Number:	Issued by:	Signature:
☐ Acknowledgement	☐ ID Card			
☐ Jurat	☐ Driver's License	**Issued Date:**	**Expiration Date:**	
☐ Oath	☐ Passport	/ /	/ /	
Other:	☐ Credible Witness	**Document Date:**	**Notary Fee:**	**Travel Fee:**
	☐ Known Personally			
	☐ _____	/ /		

Document Type:	Date/Time Notarized: / /	: AM
		: PM

Witness Full NAME: 1	Signature:	Phone No:
Address:		**Email:**
Witness Full NAME: 2	Signature:	Phone No:
Address:		**Email:**

Notes:

Signer Full NAME: | **Phone No:** | **Record No:**

Address: | **Email:** | **Thumb Print:**

Service Performed	Identification	ID Number:	Issued by:	Signature:
☐ Acknowledgement ☐ Jurat ☐ Oath Other:	☐ ID Card ☐ Driver's License ☐ Passport ☐ Credible Witness ☐ Known Personally ☐ _____	**Issued Date:** / / **Document Date:** / /	**Expiration Date:** / / **Notary Fee:**	**Travel Fee:**

Document Type: | **Date/Time Notarized:** / / | : AM
: PM

Witness Full NAME: 1	Signature:	Phone No:
Address:		Email:
Witness Full NAME: 2	Signature:	Phone No:
Address:		Email:

Notes:

Signer Full NAME: | **Phone No:** | **Record No:**

Address: | **Email:** | **Thumb Print:**

Service Performed	Identification	ID Number:	Issued by:	Signature:
☐ Acknowledgement ☐ Jurat ☐ Oath Other:	☐ ID Card ☐ Driver's License ☐ Passport ☐ Credible Witness ☐ Known Personally ☐ _____	**Issued Date:** / / **Document Date:** / /	**Expiration Date:** / / **Notary Fee:**	**Travel Fee:**

Document Type: | **Date/Time Notarized:** / / | : AM
: PM

Witness Full NAME: 1	Signature:	Phone No:
Address:		Email:
Witness Full NAME: 2	Signature:	Phone No:
Address:		Email:

Notes:

Signer Full NAME:		Phone No:		Record No:

Address: | **Email:** | **Thumb Print:**

Service Performed	Identification	ID Number:	Issued by:	Signature:
☐ Acknowledgement	☐ ID Card			
☐ Jurat	☐ Driver's License	**Issued Date:**	**Expiration Date:**	
☐ Oath	☐ Passport	/ /	/ /	
Other:	☐ Credible Witness	**Document Date:**	**Notary Fee:**	**Travel Fee:**
	☐ Known Personally	/ /		
	☐ _____			

Document Type:	Date/Time Notarized: / /	: AM
		: PM

Witness Full NAME: 1	Signature:	Phone No:
Address:		**Email:**
Witness Full NAME: 2	Signature:	Phone No:
Address:		**Email:**

Notes:

Signer Full NAME:		Phone No:		Record No:

Address: | **Email:** | **Thumb Print:**

Service Performed	Identification	ID Number:	Issued by:	Signature:
☐ Acknowledgement	☐ ID Card			
☐ Jurat	☐ Driver's License	**Issued Date:**	**Expiration Date:**	
☐ Oath	☐ Passport	/ /	/ /	
Other:	☐ Credible Witness	**Document Date:**	**Notary Fee:**	**Travel Fee:**
	☐ Known Personally	/ /		
	☐ _____			

Document Type:	Date/Time Notarized: / /	: AM
		: PM

Witness Full NAME: 1	Signature:	Phone No:
Address:		**Email:**
Witness Full NAME: 2	Signature:	Phone No:
Address:		**Email:**

Notes:

Signer Full NAME:		Phone No:		Record No:

Address: **Email:**   **Thumb Print:**

Service Performed	Identification	ID Number:	Issued by:	Signature:
☐ Acknowledgement ☐ Jurat ☐ Oath Other:	☐ ID Card ☐ Driver's License ☐ Passport ☐ Credible Witness ☐ Known Personally ☐ _____	**Issued Date:** / / **Document Date:** / /	**Expiration Date:** / / **Notary Fee:**	**Travel Fee:**

Document Type:	Date/Time Notarized: / /	: AM : PM

Witness Full NAME: 1	Signature:	Phone No:
Address:		Email:
Witness Full NAME: 2	Signature:	Phone No:
Address:		Email:

Notes:

Signer Full NAME:		Phone No:		Record No:

Address: **Email:**   **Thumb Print:**

Service Performed	Identification	ID Number:	Issued by:	Signature:
☐ Acknowledgement ☐ Jurat ☐ Oath Other:	☐ ID Card ☐ Driver's License ☐ Passport ☐ Credible Witness ☐ Known Personally ☐ _____	**Issued Date:** / / **Document Date:** / /	**Expiration Date:** / / **Notary Fee:**	**Travel Fee:**

Document Type:	Date/Time Notarized: _ / /	: AM : PM

Witness Full NAME: 1	Signature:	Phone No:
Address:		Email:
Witness Full NAME: 2	Signature:	Phone No:
Address:		Email:

Notes:

Signer Full NAME:		Phone No:		Record No:	
Address:			Email:		Thumb Print:

Service Performed	Identification	ID Number:	Issued by:	Signature:	
☐ Acknowledgement	☐ ID Card				
☐ Jurat	☐ Driver's License	Issued Date:	Expiration Date:		
☐ Oath	☐ Passport	/ /	/ /		
Other:	☐ Credible Witness	Document Date:	Notary Fee:	Travel Fee:	
	☐ Known Personally	/ /			
	☐ _____				

Document Type:	Date/Time Notarized: / /	: AM
		: PM

Witness Full NAME: 1	Signature:	Phone No:
Address:		Email:
Witness Full NAME: 2	Signature:	Phone No:
Address:		Email:

Notes:

Signer Full NAME:		Phone No:		Record No:	
Address:			Email:		Thumb Print:

Service Performed	Identification	ID Number:	Issued by:	Signature:	
☐ Acknowledgement	☐ ID Card				
☐ Jurat	☐ Driver's License	Issued Date:	Expiration Date:		
☐ Oath	☐ Passport	/ /	/ /		
Other:	☐ Credible Witness	Document Date:	Notary Fee:	Travel Fee:	
	☐ Known Personally	/ /			
	☐ _____				

Document Type:	Date/Time Notarized: / /	: AM
		: PM

Witness Full NAME: 1	Signature:	Phone No:
Address:		Email:
Witness Full NAME: 2	Signature:	Phone No:
Address:		Email:

Notes:

Signer Full NAME:		Phone No:		Record No:

Address:		Email:	Thumb Print:

Service Performed	Identification	ID Number:	Issued by:	Signature:
□ Acknowledgement	□ ID Card			
□ Jurat	□ Driver's License	**Issued Date:**	**Expiration Date:**	
□ Oath	□ Passport	/ /	/ /	
Other:	□ Credible Witness	**Document Date:**	**Notary Fee:**	**Travel Fee:**
	□ Known Personally	/ /		
	□			

Document Type:	Date/Time Notarized: / /	: AM
		: PM

Witness Full NAME: 1	Signature:	Phone No:
Address:		Email:
Witness Full NAME: 2	Signature:	Phone No:
Address:		Email:

Notes:

Signer Full NAME:		Phone No:		Record No:

Address:		Email:	Thumb Print:

Service Performed	Identification	ID Number:	Issued by:	Signature:
□ Acknowledgement	□ ID Card			
□ Jurat	□ Driver's License	**Issued Date:**	**Expiration Date:**	
□ Oath	□ Passport	/ /	/ /	
Other:	□ Credible Witness	**Document Date:**	**Notary Fee:**	**Travel Fee:**
	□ Known Personally	/ /		
	□			

Document Type:	Date/Time Notarized: / /	: AM
		: PM

Witness Full NAME: 1	Signature:	Phone No:
Address:		Email:
Witness Full NAME: 2	Signature:	Phone No:
Address:		Email:

Notes:

Signer Full NAME:		Phone No:		Record No:	
Address:			Email:		Thumb Print:

Service Performed	Identification	ID Number:	Issued by:	Signature:	
☐ Acknowledgement	☐ ID Card				
☐ Jurat	☐ Driver's License	Issued Date:	Expiration Date:		
☐ Oath	☐ Passport	/ /	/ /		
Other:	☐ Credible Witness	Document Date:	Notary Fee:	Travel Fee:	
	☐ Known Personally	/ /			
	☐ _____				

Document Type:	Date/Time Notarized: / /	: AM
		: PM

Witness Full NAME: 1	Signature:	Phone No:
Address:		Email:
Witness Full NAME: 2	Signature:	Phone No:
Address:		Email:

Notes:

Signer Full NAME:		Phone No:		Record No:	
Address:			Email:		Thumb Print:

Service Performed	Identification	ID Number:	Issued by:	Signature:	
☐ Acknowledgement	☐ ID Card				
☐ Jurat	☐ Driver's License	Issued Date:	Expiration Date:		
☐ Oath	☐ Passport	/ /	/ /		
Other:	☐ Credible Witness	Document Date:	Notary Fee:	Travel Fee:	
	☐ Known Personally	/ /			
	☐ _____				

Document Type:	Date/Time Notarized: / /	: AM
		: PM

Witness Full NAME: 1	Signature:	Phone No:
Address:		Email:
Witness Full NAME: 2	Signature:	Phone No:
Address:		Email:

Notes:

Signer Full NAME:		Phone No:		Record No:

Address:		Email:		Thumb Print:

Service Performed	Identification	ID Number:	Issued by:	Signature:
□ Acknowledgement	□ ID Card			
□ Jurat	□ Driver's License	Issued Date:	Expiration Date:	
□ Oath	□ Passport	/ /	/ /	
Other:	□ Credible Witness	Document Date:	Notary Fee:	Travel Fee:
	□ Known Personally	/ /		
	□ _____			

Document Type:	Date/Time Notarized: / /	: AM
		: PM

Witness Full NAME: 1	Signature:	Phone No:
Address:		Email:

Witness Full NAME: 2	Signature:	Phone No:
Address:		Email:

Notes:

Signer Full NAME:		Phone No:		Record No:

Address:		Email:		Thumb Print:

Service Performed	Identification	ID Number:	Issued by:	Signature:
□ Acknowledgement	□ ID Card			
□ Jurat	□ Driver's License	Issued Date:	Expiration Date:	
□ Oath	□ Passport	/ /	/ /	
Other:	□ Credible Witness	Document Date:	Notary Fee:	Travel Fee:
	□ Known Personally	/ /		
	□ _____			

Document Type:	Date/Time Notarized: / /	: AM
		: PM

Witness Full NAME: 1	Signature:	Phone No:
Address:		Email:

Witness Full NAME: 2	Signature:	Phone No:
Address:		Email:

Notes:

Signer Full NAME:		Phone No:		Record No:

Address:		Email:	Thumb Print:

Service Performed	Identification	ID Number:	Issued by:	Signature:
☐ Acknowledgement	☐ ID Card			
☐ Jurat	☐ Driver's License	Issued Date:	Expiration Date:	
☐ Oath	☐ Passport	/ /	/ /	
Other:	☐ Credible Witness	Document Date:	Notary Fee:	Travel Fee:
	☐ Known Personally			
	☐ _____	/ /		

Document Type:	Date/Time Notarized: / /	: AM
		: PM

Witness Full NAME: 1	Signature:	Phone No:
Address:		Email:
Witness Full NAME: 2	Signature:	Phone No:
Address:		Email:

Notes:

Signer Full NAME:		Phone No:		Record No:

Address:		Email:	Thumb Print:

Service Performed	Identification	ID Number:	Issued by:	Signature:
☐ Acknowledgement	☐ ID Card			
☐ Jurat	☐ Driver's License	Issued Date:	Expiration Date:	
☐ Oath	☐ Passport	/ /	/ /	
Other:	☐ Credible Witness	Document Date:	Notary Fee:	Travel Fee:
	☐ Known Personally			
	☐ _____	/ /		

Document Type:	Date/Time Notarized: / /	: AM
		: PM

Witness Full NAME: 1	Signature:	Phone No:
Address:		Email:
Witness Full NAME: 2	Signature:	Phone No:
Address:		Email:

Notes:

Signer Full NAME:		Phone No:		Record No:

Address:		Email:		Thumb Print:

Service Performed	Identification	ID Number:	Issued by:	Signature:
□ Acknowledgement □ Jurat □ Oath Other:	□ ID Card □ Driver's License □ Passport □ Credible Witness □ Known Personally □ _____	**Issued Date:** / /	**Expiration Date:** / /	
		Document Date: / /	**Notary Fee:**	**Travel Fee:**

Document Type:	Date/Time Notarized: / /	: AM : PM

Witness Full NAME: 1	Signature:	Phone No:
Address:		Email:

Witness Full NAME: 2	Signature:	Phone No:
Address:		Email:

Notes:

Signer Full NAME:		Phone No:		Record No:

Address:		Email:		Thumb Print:

Service Performed	Identification	ID Number:	Issued by:	Signature:
□ Acknowledgement □ Jurat □ Oath Other:	□ ID Card □ Driver's License □ Passport □ Credible Witness □ Known Personally □ _____	**Issued Date:** / /	**Expiration Date:** / /	
		Document Date: / /	**Notary Fee:**	**Travel Fee:**

Document Type:	Date/Time Notarized: / /	: AM : PM

Witness Full NAME: 1	Signature:	Phone No:
Address:		Email:

Witness Full NAME: 2	Signature:	Phone No:
Address:		Email:

Notes:

Signer Full NAME:		Phone No:		Record No:	
Address:			Email:		Thumb Print:

Service Performed	Identification	ID Number:	Issued by:	Signature:	
☐ Acknowledgement ☐ Jurat ☐ Oath Other:	☐ ID Card ☐ Driver's License ☐ Passport ☐ Credible Witness ☐ Known Personally ☐ _____	**Issued Date:** / /	**Expiration Date:** / /		
		Document Date: / /	**Notary Fee:**	**Travel Fee:**	

Document Type:	Date/Time Notarized: / /	:	AM
		:	PM

Witness Full NAME: 1	Signature:	Phone No:
Address:		Email:
Witness Full NAME: 2	Signature:	Phone No:
Address:		Email:

Notes:

Signer Full NAME:		Phone No:		Record No:	
Address:			Email:		Thumb Print:

Service Performed	Identification	ID Number:	Issued by:	Signature:	
☐ Acknowledgement ☐ Jurat ☐ Oath Other:	☐ ID Card ☐ Driver's License ☐ Passport ☐ Credible Witness ☐ Known Personally ☐ _____	**Issued Date:** / /	**Expiration Date:** / /		
		Document Date: / /	**Notary Fee:**	**Travel Fee:**	

Document Type:	Date/Time Notarized: / /	:	AM
		:	PM

Witness Full NAME: 1	Signature:	Phone No:
Address:		Email:
Witness Full NAME: 2	Signature:	Phone No:
Address:		Email:

Notes:

Signer Full NAME:		Phone No:		Record No:

Address:		Email:	Thumb Print:

Service Performed	Identification	ID Number:	Issued by:	Signature:
☐ Acknowledgement	☐ ID Card			
☐ Jurat	☐ Driver's License	**Issued Date:**	**Expiration Date:**	
☐ Oath	☐ Passport	/ /	/ /	
Other:	☐ Credible Witness	**Document Date:**	**Notary Fee:**	**Travel Fee:**
	☐ Known Personally			
	☐ _____	/ /		

Document Type:	Date/Time Notarized: / /	:	AM
		:	PM

Witness Full NAME: 1	Signature:	Phone No:
Address:		Email:
Witness Full NAME: 2	Signature:	Phone No:
Address:		Email:

Notes:

Signer Full NAME:		Phone No:		Record No:

Address:		Email:	Thumb Print:

Service Performed	Identification	ID Number:	Issued by:	Signature:
☐ Acknowledgement	☐ ID Card			
☐ Jurat	☐ Driver's License	**Issued Date:**	**Expiration Date:**	
☐ Oath	☐ Passport	/ /	/ /	
Other:	☐ Credible Witness	**Document Date:**	**Notary Fee:**	**Travel Fee:**
	☐ Known Personally			
	☐ _____	/ /		

Document Type:	Date/Time Notarized: / /	:	AM
		:	PM

Witness Full NAME: 1	Signature:	Phone No:
Address:		Email:
Witness Full NAME: 2	Signature:	Phone No:
Address:		Email:

Notes:

Signer Full NAME:		Phone No:		Record No:

Address: | **Email:** | **Thumb Print:**

Service Performed	Identification	ID Number:	Issued by:	Signature:
☐ Acknowledgement ☐ Jurat ☐ Oath Other:	☐ ID Card ☐ Driver's License ☐ Passport ☐ Credible Witness ☐ Known Personally ☐ _____	**Issued Date:** / /	**Expiration Date:** / /	
		Document Date: / /	**Notary Fee:**	**Travel Fee:**

Document Type:	Date/Time Notarized: / /	: AM
		: PM

Witness Full NAME: 1	Signature:	Phone No:
Address:		Email:
Witness Full NAME: 2	Signature:	Phone No:
Address:		Email:

Notes:

Signer Full NAME:		Phone No:		Record No:

Address: | **Email:** | **Thumb Print:**

Service Performed	Identification	ID Number:	Issued by:	Signature:
☐ Acknowledgement ☐ Jurat ☐ Oath Other:	☐ ID Card ☐ Driver's License ☐ Passport ☐ Credible Witness ☐ Known Personally ☐ _____	**Issued Date:** / /	**Expiration Date:** / /	
		Document Date: / /	**Notary Fee:**	**Travel Fee:**

Document Type:	Date/Time Notarized: / /	: AM
		: PM

Witness Full NAME: 1	Signature:	Phone No:
Address:		Email:
Witness Full NAME: 2	Signature:	Phone No:
Address:		Email:

Notes:

Signer Full NAME:		Phone No:		Record No:

Address:		Email:		Thumb Print:

Service Performed	Identification	ID Number:	Issued by:	Signature:
☐ Acknowledgement ☐ Jurat ☐ Oath Other:	☐ ID Card ☐ Driver's License ☐ Passport ☐ Credible Witness ☐ Known Personally ☐	**Issued Date:** / /	**Expiration Date:** / /	
		Document Date: / /	**Notary Fee:**	**Travel Fee:**

Document Type:	Date/Time Notarized: / /	: AM
		: PM

Witness Full NAME: 1	Signature:	Phone No:
Address:		Email:
Witness Full NAME: 2	Signature:	Phone No:
Address:		Email:

Notes:

Signer Full NAME:		Phone No:		Record No:

Address:		Email:		Thumb Print:

Service Performed	Identification	ID Number:	Issued by:	Signature:
☐ Acknowledgement ☐ Jurat ☐ Oath Other:	☐ ID Card ☐ Driver's License ☐ Passport ☐ Credible Witness ☐ Known Personally ☐	**Issued Date:** / /	**Expiration Date:** / /	
		Document Date: / /	**Notary Fee:**	**Travel Fee:**

Document Type:	Date/Time Notarized: / /	: AM
		: PM

Witness Full NAME: 1	Signature:	Phone No:
Address:		Email:
Witness Full NAME: 2	Signature:	Phone No:
Address:		Email:

Notes:

Signer Full NAME:		Phone No:		Record No:
Address:			Email:	Thumb Print:

Service Performed	Identification	ID Number:	Issued by:	Signature:

☐ Acknowledgement
☐ Jurat
☐ Oath
Other:
	☐ ID Card
	☐ Driver's License
	☐ Passport
	☐ Credible Witness
	☐ Known Personally
	☐ _____
		Issued Date:
		  / /
			Expiration Date:
			  / /	

		Document Date: / /	**Notary Fee:**	**Travel Fee:**

Document Type:	Date/Time Notarized: / /	: AM : PM

Witness Full NAME: 1	Signature:	Phone No:
Address:		Email:
Witness Full NAME: 2	Signature:	Phone No:
Address:		Email:

Notes:

Signer Full NAME:		Phone No:		Record No:
Address:			Email:	Thumb Print:

Service Performed	Identification	ID Number:	Issued by:	Signature:

☐ Acknowledgement
☐ Jurat
☐ Oath
Other:
	☐ ID Card
	☐ Driver's License
	☐ Passport
	☐ Credible Witness
	☐ Known Personally
	☐ _____
		Issued Date:
		  / /
			Expiration Date:
			  / /	

		Document Date: / /	**Notary Fee:**	**Travel Fee:**

Document Type:	Date/Time Notarized: / /	: AM : PM

Witness Full NAME: 1	Signature:	Phone No:
Address:		Email:
Witness Full NAME: 2	Signature:	Phone No:
Address:		Email:

Notes:

Signer Full NAME: | **Phone No:** | **Record No:**

Address: | **Email:** | **Thumb Print:**

Service Performed	Identification	ID Number:	Issued by:	Signature:
☐ Acknowledgement ☐ Jurat ☐ Oath Other:	☐ ID Card ☐ Driver's License ☐ Passport ☐ Credible Witness ☐ Known Personally ☐ _____	**Issued Date:** / /	**Expiration Date:** / /	
		Document Date: / /	**Notary Fee:**	**Travel Fee:**

Document Type: | **Date/Time Notarized:** / / | : AM
: PM

Witness Full NAME: 1	Signature:	Phone No:
Address:		Email:
Witness Full NAME: 2	Signature:	Phone No:
Address:		Email:

Notes:

Signer Full NAME: | **Phone No:** | **Record No:**

Address: | **Email:** | **Thumb Print:**

Service Performed	Identification	ID Number:	Issued by:	Signature:
☐ Acknowledgement ☐ Jurat ☐ Oath Other:	☐ ID Card ☐ Driver's License ☐ Passport ☐ Credible Witness ☐ Known Personally ☐ _____	**Issued Date:** / /	**Expiration Date:** / /	
		Document Date: / /	**Notary Fee:**	**Travel Fee:**

Document Type: | **Date/Time Notarized:** / / | : AM
: PM

Witness Full NAME: 1	Signature:	Phone No:
Address:		Email:
Witness Full NAME: 2	Signature:	Phone No:
Address:		Email:

Notes:

Signer Full NAME:		Phone No:		Record No:	

Address: | **Email:** | **Thumb Print:**

Service Performed	Identification	ID Number:	Issued by:	Signature:
☐ Acknowledgement	☐ ID Card			
☐ Jurat	☐ Driver's License	**Issued Date:**	**Expiration Date:**	
☐ Oath	☐ Passport	/ /	/ /	
Other:	☐ Credible Witness	**Document Date:**	**Notary Fee:**	**Travel Fee:**
	☐ Known Personally	/ /		
	☐ _____			

Document Type:	Date/Time Notarized: / /	: AM
		: PM

Witness Full NAME: 1	Signature:	Phone No:
Address:		Email:
Witness Full NAME: 2	Signature:	Phone No:
Address:		Email:

Notes:

Signer Full NAME:		Phone No:		Record No:	

Address: | **Email:** | **Thumb Print:**

Service Performed	Identification	ID Number:	Issued by:	Signature:
☐ Acknowledgement	☐ ID Card			
☐ Jurat	☐ Driver's License	**Issued Date:**	**Expiration Date:**	
☐ Oath	☐ Passport	/ /	/ /	
Other:	☐ Credible Witness	**Document Date:**	**Notary Fee:**	**Travel Fee:**
	☐ Known Personally	/ /		
	☐ _____			

Document Type:	Date/Time Notarized: / /	: AM
		: PM

Witness Full NAME: 1	Signature:	Phone No:
Address:		Email:
Witness Full NAME: 2	Signature:	Phone No:
Address:		Email:

Notes:

Signer Full NAME:		Phone No:		Record No:

Address: Email: Thumb Print:

Service Performed	Identification	ID Number:	Issued by:	Signature:
☐ Acknowledgement ☐ Jurat ☐ Oath Other:	☐ ID Card ☐ Driver's License ☐ Passport ☐ Credible Witness ☐ Known Personally ☐ _____	**Issued Date:** / /	**Expiration Date:** / /	
		Document Date: / /	**Notary Fee:**	**Travel Fee:**

Document Type:	Date/Time Notarized: / /	: AM : PM

Witness Full NAME: 1	Signature:	Phone No:
Address:		**Email:**
Witness Full NAME: 2	Signature:	Phone No:
Address:		**Email:**

Notes:

Signer Full NAME:		Phone No:		Record No:

Address: Email: Thumb Print:

Service Performed	Identification	ID Number:	Issued by:	Signature:
☐ Acknowledgement ☐ Jurat ☐ Oath Other:	☐ ID Card ☐ Driver's License ☐ Passport ☐ Credible Witness ☐ Known Personally ☐ _____	**Issued Date:** / /	**Expiration Date:** / /	
		Document Date: / /	**Notary Fee:**	**Travel Fee:**

Document Type:	Date/Time Notarized: / /	: AM : PM

Witness Full NAME: 1	Signature:	Phone No:
Address:		**Email:**
Witness Full NAME: 2	Signature:	Phone No:
Address:		**Email:**

Notes:

Signer Full NAME:		Phone No:		Record No:	
Address:			Email:		Thumb Print:

Service Performed	Identification	ID Number:	Issued by:	Signature:	
☐ Acknowledgement	☐ ID Card				
☐ Jurat	☐ Driver's License	Issued Date:	Expiration Date:		
☐ Oath	☐ Passport	/ /	/ /		
Other:	☐ Credible Witness	Document Date:	Notary Fee:	Travel Fee:	
	☐ Known Personally	/ /			
	☐ _____				

Document Type:	Date/Time Notarized: / /	: AM
		: PM

Witness Full NAME: 1	Signature:	Phone No:
Address:		Email:
Witness Full NAME: 2	Signature:	Phone No:
Address:		Email:

Notes:

Signer Full NAME:		Phone No:		Record No:	
Address:			Email:		Thumb Print:

Service Performed	Identification	ID Number:	Issued by:	Signature:	
☐ Acknowledgement	☐ ID Card				
☐ Jurat	☐ Driver's License	Issued Date:	Expiration Date:		
☐ Oath	☐ Passport		/ /	/ /	
Other:	☐ Credible Witness	Document Date:	Notary Fee:	Travel Fee:	
	☐ Known Personally	/ /			
	☐ _____				

Document Type:	Date/Time Notarized: / /	: AM
		: PM

Witness Full NAME: 1	Signature:	Phone No:
Address:		Email:
Witness Full NAME: 2	Signature:	Phone No:
Address:		Email:

Notes:

Signer Full NAME:		Phone No:		Record No:

Address:		Email:	Thumb Print:

Service Performed	Identification	ID Number:	Issued by:	Signature:

☐ Acknowledgement
☐ Jurat
☐ Oath
Other:
	☐ ID Card
	☐ Driver's License
	☐ Passport
	☐ Credible Witness
	☐ Known Personally
	☐ _____
		Issued Date:
		    / /
		Document Date:
		    / /
			Expiration Date:
			    / /
			Notary Fee:
				Travel Fee:

Document Type:	Date/Time Notarized: / / : AM : PM

Witness Full NAME: 1	Signature:	Phone No:
Address:		Email:

Witness Full NAME: 2	Signature:	Phone No:
Address:		Email:

Notes:

Signer Full NAME:		Phone No:		Record No:

Address:		Email:	Thumb Print:

Service Performed	Identification	ID Number:	Issued by:	Signature:

☐ Acknowledgement
☐ Jurat
☐ Oath
Other:
	☐ ID Card
	☐ Driver's License
	☐ Passport
	☐ Credible Witness
	☐ Known Personally
	☐ _____
		Issued Date:
		    / /
		Document Date:
		    / /
			Expiration Date:
			    / /
			Notary Fee:
				Travel Fee:

Document Type:	Date/Time Notarized: / / : AM : PM

Witness Full NAME: 1	Signature:	Phone No:
Address:		Email:

Witness Full NAME: 2	Signature:	Phone No:
Address:		Email:

Notes:

Signer Full NAME:		Phone No:		Record No:	

Address: **Email:**   **Thumb Print:**

Service Performed	Identification	ID Number:	Issued by:	Signature:	
☐ Acknowledgement ☐ Jurat ☐ Oath Other:	☐ ID Card ☐ Driver's License ☐ Passport ☐ Credible Witness ☐ Known Personally ☐ _____	**Issued Date:** / / **Document Date:** / /	**Expiration Date:** / / **Notary Fee:**	**Travel Fee:**	

Document Type:	Date/Time Notarized: / / : AM : PM

Witness Full NAME: 1	Signature:	Phone No:
Address:		Email:
Witness Full NAME: 2	Signature:	Phone No:
Address:		Email:

Notes:

Signer Full NAME:		Phone No:		Record No:	

Address: **Email:**   **Thumb Print:**

Service Performed	Identification	ID Number:	Issued by:	Signature:	
☐ Acknowledgement ☐ Jurat ☐ Oath Other:	☐ ID Card ☐ Driver's License ☐ Passport ☐ Credible Witness ☐ Known Personally ☐ _____	**Issued Date:** / / **Document Date:** / /	**Expiration Date:** / / **Notary Fee:**	**Travel Fee:**	

Document Type:	Date/Time Notarized: / / : AM : PM

Witness Full NAME: 1	Signature:	Phone No:
Address:		Email:
Witness Full NAME: 2	Signature:	Phone No:
Address:		Email:

Notes:

Signer Full NAME:	Phone No:	Record No:

Address:	Email:	Thumb Print:

Service Performed	Identification	ID Number:	Issued by:	Signature:
☐ Acknowledgement ☐ Jurat ☐ Oath Other:	☐ ID Card ☐ Driver's License ☐ Passport ☐ Credible Witness ☐ Known Personally ☐ _____	Issued Date: / / Document Date: / /	Expiration Date: / / Notary Fee:	Travel Fee:

Document Type:	Date/Time Notarized: / /	: AM : PM

Witness Full NAME: 1	Signature:	Phone No:
Address:		Email:

Witness Full NAME: 2	Signature:	Phone No:
Address:		Email:

Notes:

Signer Full NAME:	Phone No:	Record No:

Address:	Email:	Thumb Print:

Service Performed	Identification	ID Number:	Issued by:	Signature:
☐ Acknowledgement ☐ Jurat ☐ Oath Other:	☐ ID Card ☐ Driver's License ☐ Passport ☐ Credible Witness ☐ Known Personally ☐ _____	Issued Date: / / Document Date: / /	Expiration Date: / / Notary Fee:	Travel Fee:

Document Type:	Date/Time Notarized: / /	: AM : PM

Witness Full NAME: 1	Signature:	Phone No:
Address:		Email:

Witness Full NAME: 2	Signature:	Phone No:
Address:		Email:

Notes:

Signer Full NAME:		Phone No:		Record No:

Address: | Email: | Thumb Print:

Service Performed	Identification	ID Number:	Issued by:	Signature:
□ Acknowledgement □ Jurat □ Oath Other:	□ ID Card □ Driver's License □ Passport □ Credible Witness □ Known Personally □ _____	**Issued Date:** / / **Document Date:** / /	**Expiration Date:** / / **Notary Fee:**	**Travel Fee:**

Document Type:	Date/Time Notarized: / /	: AM : PM

Witness Full NAME: 1	Signature:	Phone No:
Address:		Email:
Witness Full NAME: 2	Signature:	Phone No:
Address:		Email:

Notes:

Signer Full NAME:		Phone No:		Record No:

Address: | Email: | Thumb Print:

Service Performed	Identification	ID Number:	Issued by:	Signature:
□ Acknowledgement □ Jurat □ Oath Other:	□ ID Card □ Driver's License □ Passport □ Credible Witness □ Known Personally □ _____	**Issued Date:** / / **Document Date:** / /	**Expiration Date:** / / **Notary Fee:**	**Travel Fee:**

Document Type:	Date/Time Notarized: / /	: AM : PM

Witness Full NAME: 1	Signature:	Phone No:
Address:		Email:
Witness Full NAME: 2	Signature:	Phone No:
Address:		Email:

Notes:

Signer Full NAME:		Phone No:		Record No:	

Address: | Email: | Thumb Print:

Service Performed	Identification	ID Number:	Issued by:	Signature:
☐ Acknowledgement	☐ ID Card			
☐ Jurat	☐ Driver's License	**Issued Date:**	**Expiration Date:**	
☐ Oath	☐ Passport	/ /	/ /	
Other:	☐ Credible Witness	**Document Date:**	**Notary Fee:**	**Travel Fee:**
	☐ Known Personally			
	☐	/ /		

Document Type:	Date/Time Notarized: / /	: AM
		: PM

Witness Full NAME: 1	Signature:	Phone No:
Address:		Email:
Witness Full NAME: 2	Signature:	Phone No:
Address:		Email:

Notes:

Signer Full NAME:		Phone No:		Record No:	

Address: | Email: | Thumb Print:

Service Performed	Identification	ID Number:	Issued by:	Signature:
☐ Acknowledgement	☐ ID Card			
☐ Jurat	☐ Driver's License	**Issued Date:**	**Expiration Date:**	
☐ Oath	☐ Passport	/ /	/ /	
Other:	☐ Credible Witness	**Document Date:**	**Notary Fee:**	**Travel Fee:**
	☐ Known Personally			
	☐	/ /		

Document Type:	Date/Time Notarized: / /	: AM
		: PM

Witness Full NAME: 1	Signature:	Phone No:
Address:		Email:
Witness Full NAME: 2	Signature:	Phone No:
Address:		Email:

Notes:

Signer Full NAME:		Phone No:		Record No:

Address:		Email:	Thumb Print:

Service Performed
- ☐ Acknowledgement
- ☐ Jurat
- ☐ Oath
- Other:

Identification
- ☐ ID Card
- ☐ Driver's License
- ☐ Passport
- ☐ Credible Witness
- ☐ Known Personally
- ☐ _____

ID Number:	Issued by:	Signature:
Issued Date: / /	Expiration Date: / /	
Document Date: / /	Notary Fee:	Travel Fee:

Document Type:	Date/Time Notarized: / /	: AM
		: PM

Witness Full NAME: 1	Signature:	Phone No:
Address:		Email:

Witness Full NAME: 2	Signature:	Phone No:
Address:		Email:

Notes:

Signer Full NAME:		Phone No:		Record No:

Address:		Email:	Thumb Print:

Service Performed
- ☐ Acknowledgement
- ☐ Jurat
- ☐ Oath
- Other:

Identification
- ☐ ID Card
- ☐ Driver's License
- ☐ Passport
- ☐ Credible Witness
- ☐ Known Personally
- ☐ _____

ID Number:	Issued by:	Signature:
Issued Date: / /	Expiration Date: / /	
Document Date: / /	Notary Fee:	Travel Fee:

Document Type:	Date/Time Notarized: / /	: AM
		: PM

Witness Full NAME: 1	Signature:	Phone No:
Address:		Email:

Witness Full NAME: 2	Signature:	Phone No:
Address:		Email:

Notes:

Signer Full NAME:		Phone No:		Record No:

Address: Email: Thumb Print:

Service Performed	Identification	ID Number:	Issued by:	Signature:
☐ Acknowledgement	☐ ID Card			
☐ Jurat	☐ Driver's License	**Issued Date:**	**Expiration Date:**	
☐ Oath	☐ Passport	/ /	/ /	
Other:	☐ Credible Witness	**Document Date:**	**Notary Fee:**	**Travel Fee:**
	☐ Known Personally	/ /		
	☐ ____			

Document Type:	Date/Time Notarized: / / : AM
	: PM

Witness Full NAME: 1	Signature:	Phone No:
Address:		Email:
Witness Full NAME: 2	Signature:	Phone No:
Address:		Email:

Notes:

Signer Full NAME:		Phone No:		Record No:

Address: Email: Thumb Print:

Service Performed	Identification	ID Number:	Issued by:	Signature:
☐ Acknowledgement	☐ ID Card			
☐ Jurat	☐ Driver's License	**Issued Date:**	**Expiration Date:**	
☐ Oath	☐ Passport	/ /	/ /	
Other:	☐ Credible Witness	**Document Date:**	**Notary Fee:**	**Travel Fee:**
	☐ Known Personally	/ /		
	☐ ____			

Document Type:	Date/Time Notarized: / / : AM
	: PM

Witness Full NAME: 1	Signature:	Phone No:
Address:		Email:
Witness Full NAME: 2	Signature:	Phone No:
Address:		Email:

Notes:

Signer Full NAME:		Phone No:		Record No:	
Address:		Email:			Thumb Print:

Service Performed	Identification	ID Number:	Issued by:	Signature:	
☐ Acknowledgement	☐ ID Card				
☐ Jurat	☐ Driver's License	Issued Date:	Expiration Date:		
☐ Oath	☐ Passport	/ /	/ /		
Other:	☐ Credible Witness	Document Date:	Notary Fee:	Travel Fee:	
	☐ Known Personally	/ /			
	☐ _____				

Document Type:	Date/Time Notarized: / /	: AM
		: PM

Witness Full NAME: 1	Signature:	Phone No:
Address:		Email:
Witness Full NAME: 2	Signature:	Phone No:
Address:		Email:

Notes:

Signer Full NAME:		Phone No:		Record No:	
Address:		Email:			Thumb Print:

Service Performed	Identification	ID Number:	Issued by:	Signature:	
☐ Acknowledgement	☐ ID Card				
☐ Jurat	☐ Driver's License	Issued Date:	Expiration Date:		
☐ Oath	☐ Passport	/ /	/ /		
Other:	☐ Credible Witness	Document Date:	Notary Fee:	Travel Fee:	
	☐ Known Personally	/ /			
	☐ _____				

Document Type:	Date/Time Notarized: / /	: AM
		: PM

Witness Full NAME: 1	Signature:	Phone No:
Address:		Email:
Witness Full NAME: 2	Signature:	Phone No:
Address:		Email:

Notes:

Signer Full NAME:		Phone No:		Record No:	

Address: | **Email:** | **Thumb Print:**

Service Performed	Identification	ID Number:	Issued by:	Signature:	
☐ Acknowledgement ☐ Jurat ☐ Oath Other:	☐ ID Card ☐ Driver's License ☐ Passport ☐ Credible Witness ☐ Known Personally ☐ _____	**Issued Date:** / /	**Expiration Date:** / /		
		Document Date: / /	**Notary Fee:**	**Travel Fee:**	

Document Type:	Date/Time Notarized: / /	: AM : PM

Witness Full NAME: 1	Signature:	Phone No:
Address:		Email:
Witness Full NAME: 2	Signature:	Phone No:
Address:		Email:

Notes:

Signer Full NAME:		Phone No:		Record No:	

Address: | **Email:** | **Thumb Print:**

Service Performed	Identification	ID Number:	Issued by:	Signature:	
☐ Acknowledgement ☐ Jurat ☐ Oath Other:	☐ ID Card ☐ Driver's License ☐ Passport ☐ Credible Witness ☐ Known Personally ☐ _____	**Issued Date:** / /	**Expiration Date:** / /		
		Document Date: / /	**Notary Fee:**	**Travel Fee:**	

Document Type:	Date/Time Notarized: / /	: AM : PM

Witness Full NAME: 1	Signature:	Phone No:
Address:		Email:
Witness Full NAME: 2	Signature:	Phone No:
Address:		Email:

Notes:

Signer Full NAME:		Phone No:		Record No:	
Address:			Email:		Thumb Print:

Service Performed	Identification	ID Number:	Issued by:	Signature:	
☐ Acknowledgement	☐ ID Card				
☐ Jurat	☐ Driver's License	Issued Date:	Expiration Date:		
☐ Oath	☐ Passport	/ /	/ /		
Other:	☐ Credible Witness	Document Date:	Notary Fee:	Travel Fee:	
	☐ Known Personally	/ /			
	☐ _____				

Document Type:	Date/Time Notarized: / /	: AM
		: PM

Witness Full NAME: 1	Signature:	Phone No:
Address:		Email:
Witness Full NAME: 2	Signature:	Phone No:
Address:		Email:

Notes:

Signer Full NAME:		Phone No:		Record No:	
Address:			Email:		Thumb Print:

Service Performed	Identification	ID Number:	Issued by:	Signature:	
☐ Acknowledgement	☐ ID Card				
☐ Jurat	☐ Driver's License	Issued Date:	Expiration Date:		
☐ Oath	☐ Passport	/ /	/ /		
Other:	☐ Credible Witness	Document Date:	Notary Fee:	Travel Fee:	
	☐ Known Personally	/ /			
	☐ _____				

Document Type:	Date/Time Notarized: / /	: AM
		: PM

Witness Full NAME: 1	Signature:	Phone No:
Address:		Email:
Witness Full NAME: 2	Signature:	Phone No:
Address:		Email:

Notes:

Record 1

Signer Full NAME:		Phone No:		Record No:

Address:		Email:		Thumb Print:

Service Performed	Identification	ID Number:	Issued by:	Signature:
□ Acknowledgement □ Jurat □ Oath Other:	□ ID Card □ Driver's License □ Passport □ Credible Witness □ Known Personally □ _____	**Issued Date:** / /	**Expiration Date:** / /	
		Document Date: / /	**Notary Fee:**	**Travel Fee:**

Document Type:	Date/Time Notarized: / /	: AM : PM

Witness Full NAME: 1	Signature:	Phone No:
Address:		Email:
Witness Full NAME: 2	Signature:	Phone No:
Address:		Email:

Notes:

Record 2

Signer Full NAME:		Phone No:		Record No:

Address:		Email:		Thumb Print:

Service Performed	Identification	ID Number:	Issued by:	Signature:
□ Acknowledgement □ Jurat □ Oath Other:	□ ID Card □ Driver's License □ Passport □ Credible Witness □ Known Personally □ _____	**Issued Date:** / /	**Expiration Date:** / /	
		Document Date: / /	**Notary Fee:**	**Travel Fee:**

Document Type:	Date/Time Notarized: / /	: AM : PM

Witness Full NAME: 1	Signature:	Phone No:
Address:		Email:
Witness Full NAME: 2	Signature:	Phone No:
Address:		Email:

Notes:

Signer Full NAME:		Phone No:		Record No:

Address: Email: Thumb Print:

Service Performed	Identification	ID Number:	Issued by:	Signature:
☐ Acknowledgement	☐ ID Card			
☐ Jurat	☐ Driver's License	**Issued Date:**	**Expiration Date:**	
☐ Oath	☐ Passport	/ /	/ /	
Other:	☐ Credible Witness	**Document Date:**	**Notary Fee:**	**Travel Fee:**
	☐ Known Personally	/ /		
	☐ _____			

Document Type:	Date/Time Notarized: / /	: AM
		: PM

Witness Full NAME: 1	Signature:	Phone No:
Address:		**Email:**
Witness Full NAME: 2	Signature:	Phone No:
Address:		**Email:**

Notes:

Signer Full NAME:		Phone No:		Record No:

Address: Email: Thumb Print:

Service Performed	Identification	ID Number:	Issued by:	Signature:
☐ Acknowledgement	☐ ID Card			
☐ Jurat	☐ Driver's License	**Issued Date:**	**Expiration Date:**	
☐ Oath	☐ Passport	/ /	/ /	
Other:	☐ Credible Witness	**Document Date:**	**Notary Fee:**	**Travel Fee:**
	☐ Known Personally	/ /		
	☐ _____			

Document Type:	Date/Time Notarized: / /	: AM
		: PM

Witness Full NAME: 1	Signature:	Phone No:
Address:		**Email:**
Witness Full NAME: 2	Signature:	Phone No:
Address:		**Email:**

Notes:

Signer Full NAME:		Phone No:		Record No:

Address: **Email:**   **Thumb Print:**

Service Performed	Identification	ID Number:	Issued by:	Signature:
☐ Acknowledgement ☐ Jurat ☐ Oath Other:	☐ ID Card ☐ Driver's License ☐ Passport ☐ Credible Witness ☐ Known Personally ☐ _____	**Issued Date:** / /	**Expiration Date:** / /	
		Document Date: / /	**Notary Fee:**	**Travel Fee:**

Document Type:	Date/Time Notarized: / /	: AM
		: PM

Witness Full NAME: 1	Signature:	Phone No:
Address:		Email:
Witness Full NAME: 2	Signature:	Phone No:
Address:		Email:

Notes:

Signer Full NAME:		Phone No:		Record No:

Address: **Email:**   **Thumb Print:**

Service Performed	Identification	ID Number:	Issued by:	Signature:
☐ Acknowledgement ☐ Jurat ☐ Oath Other:	☐ ID Card ☐ Driver's License ☐ Passport ☐ Credible Witness ☐ Known Personally ☐ _____	**Issued Date:** / /	**Expiration Date:** / /	
		Document Date: / /	**Notary Fee:**	**Travel Fee:**

Document Type:	Date/Time Notarized: / /	: AM
		: PM

Witness Full NAME: 1	Signature:	Phone No:
Address:		Email:
Witness Full NAME: 2	Signature:	Phone No:
Address:		Email:

Notes:

Signer Full NAME:		Phone No:		Record No:

Address: | **Email:** | **Thumb Print:**

Service Performed	Identification	ID Number:	Issued by:	Signature:
□ Acknowledgement	□ ID Card			
□ Jurat	□ Driver's License	**Issued Date:**	**Expiration Date:**	
□ Oath	□ Passport	/ /	/ /	
Other:	□ Credible Witness	**Document Date:**	**Notary Fee:**	**Travel Fee:**
	□ Known Personally	/ /		
	□ _____			

Document Type:	Date/Time Notarized: / /	: AM
		: PM

Witness Full NAME: 1	Signature:	Phone No:
Address:		**Email:**
Witness Full NAME: 2	**Signature:**	**Phone No:**
Address:		**Email:**

Notes:

Signer Full NAME:		Phone No:		Record No:

Address: | **Email:** | **Thumb Print:**

Service Performed	Identification	ID Number:	Issued by:	Signature:
□ Acknowledgement	□ ID Card			
□ Jurat	□ Driver's License	**Issued Date:**	**Expiration Date:**	
□ Oath	□ Passport	/ /	/ /	
Other:	□ Credible Witness	**Document Date:**	**Notary Fee:**	**Travel Fee:**
	□ Known Personally	/ /		
	□ _____			

Document Type:	Date/Time Notarized: / /	: AM
		: PM

Witness Full NAME: 1	Signature:	Phone No:
Address:		**Email:**
Witness Full NAME: 2	**Signature:**	**Phone No:**
Address:		**Email:**

Notes:

Signer Full NAME: | **Phone No:** | **Record No:**

Address: | **Email:** | **Thumb Print:**

Service Performed	Identification	ID Number:	Issued by:	Signature:
☐ Acknowledgement ☐ Jurat ☐ Oath Other:	☐ ID Card ☐ Driver's License ☐ Passport ☐ Credible Witness ☐ Known Personally ☐ _____	**Issued Date:** / /	**Expiration Date:** / /	
		Document Date: / /	**Notary Fee:**	**Travel Fee:**

Document Type: | **Date/Time Notarized:** / / | : AM
: PM

Witness Full NAME: 1	Signature:	Phone No:
Address:		Email:
Witness Full NAME: 2	Signature:	Phone No:
Address:		Email:

Notes:

Signer Full NAME: | **Phone No:** | **Record No:**

Address: | **Email:** | **Thumb Print:**

Service Performed	Identification	ID Number:	Issued by:	Signature:
☐ Acknowledgement ☐ Jurat ☐ Oath Other:	☐ ID Card ☐ Driver's License ☐ Passport ☐ Credible Witness ☐ Known Personally ☐ _____	**Issued Date:** / /	**Expiration Date:** / /	
		Document Date: / /	**Notary Fee:**	**Travel Fee:**

Document Type: | **Date/Time Notarized:** / / | : AM
: PM

Witness Full NAME: 1	Signature:	Phone No:
Address:		Email:
Witness Full NAME: 2	Signature:	Phone No:
Address:		Email:

Notes:

Signer Full NAME:		Phone No:		Record No:	
Address:			Email:		Thumb Print:

Service Performed	Identification	ID Number:	Issued by:	Signature:	
☐ Acknowledgement ☐ Jurat ☐ Oath Other:	☐ ID Card ☐ Driver's License ☐ Passport ☐ Credible Witness ☐ Known Personally ☐ _____	Issued Date: / /	Expiration Date: / /		
		Document Date: / /	Notary Fee:	Travel Fee:	

Document Type:	Date/Time Notarized: / /	: AM : PM

Witness Full NAME: 1	Signature:	Phone No:
Address:		Email:
Witness Full NAME: 2	Signature:	Phone No:
Address:		Email:

Notes:

Signer Full NAME:		Phone No:		Record No:	
Address:			Email:		Thumb Print:

Service Performed	Identification	ID Number:	Issued by:	Signature:	
☐ Acknowledgement ☐ Jurat ☐ Oath Other:	☐ ID Card ☐ Driver's License ☐ Passport ☐ Credible Witness ☐ Known Personally ☐ _____	Issued Date: / /	Expiration Date: / /		
		Document Date: / /	Notary Fee:	Travel Fee:	

Document Type:	Date/Time Notarized: / /	: AM : PM

Witness Full NAME: 1	Signature:	Phone No:
Address:		Email:
Witness Full NAME: 2	Signature:	Phone No:
Address:		Email:

Notes:

Signer Full NAME:		Phone No:		Record No:
Address:			Email:	Thumb Print:

Service Performed	Identification	ID Number:	Issued by:	Signature:
☐ Acknowledgement ☐ Jurat ☐ Oath Other:	☐ ID Card ☐ Driver's License ☐ Passport ☐ Credible Witness ☐ Known Personally ☐ _____	**Issued Date:** / / **Document Date:** / /	**Expiration Date:** / / **Notary Fee:**	**Travel Fee:**

Document Type:	Date/Time Notarized: / /	: AM
		: PM

Witness Full NAME: 1	Signature:	Phone No:
Address:		Email:
Witness Full NAME: 2	Signature:	Phone No:
Address:		Email:

Notes:

Signer Full NAME:		Phone No:		Record No:
Address:			Email:	Thumb Print:

Service Performed	Identification	ID Number:	Issued by:	Signature:
☐ Acknowledgement ☐ Jurat ☐ Oath Other:	☐ ID Card ☐ Driver's License ☐ Passport ☐ Credible Witness ☐ Known Personally ☐ _____	**Issued Date:** / / **Document Date:** / /	**Expiration Date:** / / **Notary Fee:**	**Travel Fee:**

Document Type:	Date/Time Notarized: / /	: AM
		: PM

Witness Full NAME: 1	Signature:	Phone No:
Address:		Email:
Witness Full NAME: 2	Signature:	Phone No:
Address:		Email:

Notes:

Record 1

Signer Full NAME:		Phone No:		Record No:	

Address: Email: Thumb Print:

Service Performed	Identification	ID Number:	Issued by:	Signature:
☐ Acknowledgement	☐ ID Card			
☐ Jurat	☐ Driver's License	Issued Date: / /	Expiration Date: / /	
☐ Oath	☐ Passport			
Other:	☐ Credible Witness			
	☐ Known Personally	Document Date: / /	Notary Fee:	Travel Fee:
	☐ _____			

Document Type: Date/Time Notarized: / /   :   AM   :   PM

Witness Full NAME: 1	Signature:	Phone No:
Address:		Email:
Witness Full NAME: 2	Signature:	Phone No:
Address:		Email:

Notes:

Record 2

Signer Full NAME:		Phone No:		Record No:	

Address: Email: Thumb Print:

Service Performed	Identification	ID Number:	Issued by:	Signature:
☐ Acknowledgement	☐ ID Card			
☐ Jurat	☐ Driver's License	Issued Date: / /	Expiration Date: / /	
☐ Oath	☐ Passport			
Other:	☐ Credible Witness			
	☐ Known Personally	Document Date: / /	Notary Fee:	Travel Fee:
	☐ _____			

Document Type: Date/Time Notarized: / /   :   AM   :   PM

Witness Full NAME: 1	Signature:	Phone No:
Address:		Email:
Witness Full NAME: 2	Signature:	Phone No:
Address:		Email:

Notes:

Signer Full NAME:		Phone No:		Record No:

Address:		Email:	Thumb Print:

Service Performed	Identification	ID Number:	Issued by:	Signature:
□ Acknowledgement	□ ID Card			
□ Jurat	□ Driver's License	**Issued Date:**	**Expiration Date:**	
□ Oath	□ Passport	/ /	/ /	
Other:	□ Credible Witness	**Document Date:**	**Notary Fee:**	**Travel Fee:**
	□ Known Personally	/ /		
	□ _____			

Document Type:	Date/Time Notarized: / /	: AM
		: PM

Witness Full NAME: 1	Signature:	Phone No:
Address:		Email:
Witness Full NAME: 2	Signature:	Phone No:
Address:		Email:

Notes:

Signer Full NAME:		Phone No:		Record No:

Address:		Email:	Thumb Print:

Service Performed	Identification	ID Number:	Issued by:	Signature:
□ Acknowledgement	□ ID Card			
□ Jurat	□ Driver's License	**Issued Date:**	**Expiration Date:**	
□ Oath	□ Passport	/ /	/ /	
Other:	□ Credible Witness	**Document Date:**	**Notary Fee:**	**Travel Fee:**
	□ Known Personally	/ /		
	□ _____			

Document Type:	Date/Time Notarized: / /	: AM
		: PM

Witness Full NAME: 1	Signature:	Phone No:
Address:		Email:
Witness Full NAME: 2	Signature:	Phone No:
Address:		Email:

Notes:

Signer Full NAME:		Phone No:		Record No:

Address:		Email:	Thumb Print:

Service Performed	Identification	ID Number:	Issued by:	Signature:
☐ Acknowledgement ☐ Jurat ☐ Oath Other:	☐ ID Card ☐ Driver's License ☐ Passport ☐ Credible Witness ☐ Known Personally ☐ _____	Issued Date: / /	Expiration Date: / /	
		Document Date: / /	Notary Fee:	Travel Fee:

Document Type:	Date/Time Notarized: / /	: AM : PM

Witness Full NAME: 1	Signature:	Phone No:
Address:		Email:
Witness Full NAME: 2	Signature:	Phone No:
Address:		Email:

Notes:

Signer Full NAME:		Phone No:		Record No:

Address:		Email:	Thumb Print:

Service Performed	Identification	ID Number:	Issued by:	Signature:
☐ Acknowledgement ☐ Jurat ☐ Oath Other:	☐ ID Card ☐ Driver's License ☐ Passport ☐ Credible Witness ☐ Known Personally ☐ _____	Issued Date: / /	Expiration Date: / /	
		Document Date: / /	Notary Fee:	Travel Fee:

Document Type:	Date/Time Notarized: / /	: AM : PM

Witness Full NAME: 1	Signature:	Phone No:
Address:		Email:
Witness Full NAME: 2	Signature:	Phone No:
Address:		Email:

Notes:

Signer Full NAME:		Phone No:		Record No:

Address:		Email:	Thumb Print:

Service Performed	Identification	ID Number:	Issued by:	Signature:
☐ Acknowledgement	☐ ID Card			
☐ Jurat	☐ Driver's License	Issued Date:	Expiration Date:	
☐ Oath	☐ Passport	/ /	/ /	
Other:	☐ Credible Witness	Document Date:	Notary Fee:	Travel Fee:
	☐ Known Personally	/ /		
	☐ _____			

Document Type:	Date/Time Notarized: / /	: AM
		: PM

Witness Full NAME: 1	Signature:	Phone No:
Address:		Email:
Witness Full NAME: 2	Signature:	Phone No:
Address:		Email:

Notes:

Signer Full NAME:		Phone No:		Record No:

Address:		Email:	Thumb Print:

Service Performed	Identification	ID Number:	Issued by:	Signature:
☐ Acknowledgement	☐ ID Card			
☐ Jurat	☐ Driver's License	Issued Date:	Expiration Date:	
☐ Oath	☐ Passport	/ /	/ /	
Other:	☐ Credible Witness	Document Date:	Notary Fee:	Travel Fee:
	☐ Known Personally	/ /		
	☐ _____			

Document Type:	Date/Time Notarized: / /	: AM
		: PM

Witness Full NAME: 1	Signature:	Phone No:
Address:		Email:
Witness Full NAME: 2	Signature:	Phone No:
Address:		Email:

Notes:

Signer Full NAME:		Phone No:		Record No:	

Address: **Email:**   **Thumb Print:**

Service Performed	Identification	ID Number:	Issued by:	Signature:

☐ Acknowledgement
☐ Jurat
☐ Oath
Other:
	☐ ID Card
	☐ Driver's License
	☐ Passport
	☐ Credible Witness
	☐ Known Personally
	☐ _____
		Issued Date:
		  / /
			Expiration Date:
			  / /	

		Document Date: / /	**Notary Fee:**	**Travel Fee:**

Document Type: **Date/Time Notarized:**   / /   :   AM   :   PM

Witness Full NAME: 1	Signature:	Phone No:
Address:		**Email:**
Witness Full NAME: 2	Signature:	Phone No:
Address:		**Email:**

Notes:

Signer Full NAME:		Phone No:		Record No:	

Address: **Email:**   **Thumb Print:**

Service Performed	Identification	ID Number:	Issued by:	Signature:

☐ Acknowledgement
☐ Jurat
☐ Oath
Other:
	☐ ID Card
	☐ Driver's License
	☐ Passport
	☐ Credible Witness
	☐ Known Personally
	☐ _____
		Issued Date:
		  / /
			Expiration Date:
			  / /	

		Document Date: / /	**Notary Fee:**	**Travel Fee:**

Document Type: **Date/Time Notarized:**   / /   :   AM   :   PM

Witness Full NAME: 1	Signature:	Phone No:
Address:		**Email:**
Witness Full NAME: 2	Signature:	Phone No:
Address:		**Email:**

Notes:

Signer Full NAME:		Phone No:		Record No:

Address: | Email: | Thumb Print:

Service Performed	Identification	ID Number:	Issued by:	Signature:
☐ Acknowledgement ☐ Jurat ☐ Oath Other:	☐ ID Card ☐ Driver's License ☐ Passport ☐ Credible Witness ☐ Known Personally ☐ _____	**Issued Date:** / /	**Expiration Date:** / /	
		Document Date: / /	**Notary Fee:**	**Travel Fee:**

Document Type:	Date/Time Notarized: / /	: AM : PM

Witness Full NAME: 1	Signature:	Phone No:
Address:		Email:
Witness Full NAME: 2	Signature:	Phone No:
Address:		Email:

Notes:

Signer Full NAME:		Phone No:		Record No:

Address: | Email: | Thumb Print:

Service Performed	Identification	ID Number:	Issued by:	Signature:
☐ Acknowledgement ☐ Jurat ☐ Oath Other:	☐ ID Card ☐ Driver's License ☐ Passport ☐ Credible Witness ☐ Known Personally ☐ _____	**Issued Date:** / /	**Expiration Date:** / /	
		Document Date: / /	**Notary Fee:**	**Travel Fee:**

Document Type:	Date/Time Notarized: / /	: AM : PM

Witness Full NAME: 1	Signature:	Phone No:
Address:		Email:
Witness Full NAME: 2	Signature:	Phone No:
Address:		Email:

Notes:

Signer Full NAME:		Phone No:		Record No:	

Address: | **Email:** | **Thumb Print:**

Service Performed	Identification	ID Number:	Issued by:	Signature:
☐ Acknowledgement	☐ ID Card			
☐ Jurat	☐ Driver's License	**Issued Date:**	**Expiration Date:**	
☐ Oath	☐ Passport	/ /	/ /	
Other:	☐ Credible Witness	**Document Date:**	**Notary Fee:**	**Travel Fee:**
	☐ Known Personally			
	☐ _____	/ /		

Document Type:	Date/Time Notarized: / /	: AM
		: PM

Witness Full NAME: 1	Signature:	Phone No:
Address:		Email:
Witness Full NAME: 2	Signature:	Phone No:
Address:		Email:

Notes:

Signer Full NAME:		Phone No:		Record No:	

Address: | **Email:** | **Thumb Print:**

Service Performed	Identification	ID Number:	Issued by:	Signature:
☐ Acknowledgement	☐ ID Card			
☐ Jurat	☐ Driver's License	**Issued Date:**	**Expiration Date:**	
☐ Oath	☐ Passport	/ /	/ /	
Other:	☐ Credible Witness	**Document Date:**	**Notary Fee:**	**Travel Fee:**
	☐ Known Personally			
	☐ _____	/ /		

Document Type:	Date/Time Notarized: / /	: AM
		: PM

Witness Full NAME: 1	Signature:	Phone No:
Address:		Email:
Witness Full NAME: 2	Signature:	Phone No:
Address:		Email:

Notes:

Signer Full NAME: | **Phone No:** | **Record No:**

Address: | **Email:** | **Thumb Print:**

Service Performed	**Identification**	**ID Number:**	**Issued by:**	**Signature:**
☐ Acknowledgement	☐ ID Card			
☐ Jurat	☐ Driver's License	**Issued Date:**	**Expiration Date:**	
☐ Oath	☐ Passport	/ /	/ /	
Other:	☐ Credible Witness	**Document Date:**	**Notary Fee:**	**Travel Fee:**
	☐ Known Personally	/ /		
	☐ _____			

Document Type:	**Date/Time Notarized:** / /	: AM
		: PM

Witness Full NAME: 1	**Signature:**	**Phone No:**
Address:		**Email:**
Witness Full NAME: 2	**Signature:**	**Phone No:**
Address:		**Email:**

Notes:

Signer Full NAME: | **Phone No:** | **Record No:**

Address: | **Email:** | **Thumb Print:**

Service Performed	**Identification**	**ID Number:**	**Issued by:**	**Signature:**
☐ Acknowledgement	☐ ID Card			
☐ Jurat	☐ Driver's License	**Issued Date:**	**Expiration Date:**	
☐ Oath	☐ Passport	/ /	/ /	
Other:	☐ Credible Witness	**Document Date:**	**Notary Fee:**	**Travel Fee:**
	☐ Known Personally	/ /		
	☐			

Document Type:	**Date/Time Notarized:** / /	: AM
		: PM

Witness Full NAME: 1	**Signature:**	**Phone No:**
Address:		**Email:**
Witness Full NAME: 2	**Signature:**	**Phone No:**
Address:		**Email:**

Notes:

Signer Full NAME:		Phone No:		Record No:	
Address:			Email:	Thumb Print:	

Service Performed	Identification	ID Number:	Issued by:	Signature:	

☐ Acknowledgement
☐ Jurat
☐ Oath
Other:
	☐ ID Card
	☐ Driver's License
	☐ Passport
	☐ Credible Witness
	☐ Known Personally
	☐ _____
		Issued Date:
		  / /
			Expiration Date:
			  / /		

		Document Date: / /	Notary Fee:	Travel Fee:	

Document Type:	Date/Time Notarized: / /	: AM : PM

Witness Full NAME: 1	Signature:	Phone No:
Address:		Email:
Witness Full NAME: 2	Signature:	Phone No:
Address:		Email:

Notes:

Signer Full NAME:		Phone No:		Record No:	
Address:			Email:	Thumb Print:	

Service Performed	Identification	ID Number:	Issued by:	Signature:	

☐ Acknowledgement
☐ Jurat
☐ Oath
Other:
	☐ ID Card
	☐ Driver's License
	☐ Passport
	☐ Credible Witness
	☐ Known Personally
	☐ _____
		Issued Date:
		  / /
			Expiration Date:
			  / /		

		Document Date: / /	Notary Fee:	Travel Fee:	

Document Type:	Date/Time Notarized: / /	: AM : PM

Witness Full NAME: 1	Signature:	Phone No:
Address:		Email:
Witness Full NAME: 2	Signature:	Phone No:
Address:		Email:

Notes:

Signer Full NAME:		Phone No:		Record No:	
Address:			Email:		Thumb Print:

Service Performed	Identification	ID Number:	Issued by:	Signature:
□ Acknowledgement □ Jurat □ Oath Other:	□ ID Card □ Driver's License □ Passport □ Credible Witness □ Known Personally □ _____	**Issued Date:** / /	**Expiration Date:** / /	
		Document Date: / /	**Notary Fee:**	**Travel Fee:**

Document Type:	Date/Time Notarized: / /	: AM : PM

Witness Full NAME: 1	Signature:	Phone No:
Address:		Email:
Witness Full NAME: 2	Signature:	Phone No:
Address:		Email:

Notes:

Signer Full NAME:		Phone No:		Record No:	
Address:			Email:		Thumb Print:

Service Performed	Identification	ID Number:	Issued by:	Signature:
□ Acknowledgement □ Jurat □ Oath Other:	□ ID Card □ Driver's License □ Passport □ Credible Witness □ Known Personally □ _____	**Issued Date:** / /	**Expiration Date:** / /	
		Document Date: / /	**Notary Fee:**	**Travel Fee:**

Document Type:	Date/Time Notarized: / /	: AM : PM

Witness Full NAME: 1	Signature:	Phone No:
Address:		Email:
Witness Full NAME: 2	Signature:	Phone No:
Address:		Email:

Notes:

Signer Full NAME:		Phone No:		Record No:

Address:		Email:		Thumb Print:

Service Performed	Identification	ID Number:	Issued by:	Signature:
☐ Acknowledgement	☐ ID Card			
☐ Jurat	☐ Driver's License	**Issued Date:**	**Expiration Date:**	
☐ Oath	☐ Passport	/ /	/ /	
Other:	☐ Credible Witness	**Document Date:**	**Notary Fee:**	**Travel Fee:**
	☐ Known Personally			
	☐ _____	/ /		

Document Type:	Date/Time Notarized: / /	: AM
		: PM

Witness Full NAME: 1	Signature:	Phone No:
Address:		Email:
Witness Full NAME: 2	Signature:	Phone No:
Address:		Email:

Notes:

Signer Full NAME:		Phone No:		Record No:

Address:		Email:		Thumb Print:

Service Performed	Identification	ID Number:	Issued by:	Signature:
☐ Acknowledgement	☐ ID Card			
☐ Jurat	☐ Driver's License	**Issued Date:**	**Expiration Date:**	
☐ Oath	☐ Passport	/ /	/ /	
Other:	☐ Credible Witness	**Document Date:**	**Notary Fee:**	**Travel Fee:**
	☐ Known Personally			
	☐ _____	/ /		

Document Type:	Date/Time Notarized: / /	: AM
		: PM

Witness Full NAME: 1	Signature:	Phone No:
Address:		Email:
Witness Full NAME: 2	Signature:	Phone No:
Address:		Email:

Notes:

Signer Full NAME:		Phone No:		Record No:	
Address:			Email:		Thumb Print:

Service Performed	Identification	ID Number:	Issued by:	Signature:	
☐ Acknowledgement	☐ ID Card				
☐ Jurat	☐ Driver's License	Issued Date:	Expiration Date:		
☐ Oath	☐ Passport	/ /	/ /		
Other:	☐ Credible Witness	Document Date:	Notary Fee:	Travel Fee:	
	☐ Known Personally	/ /			
	☐ _____				

Document Type:	Date/Time Notarized: / /	: AM
		: PM

Witness Full NAME: 1	Signature:	Phone No:
Address:		Email:

Witness Full NAME: 2	Signature:	Phone No:
Address:		Email:

Notes:

Signer Full NAME:		Phone No:		Record No:	
Address:			Email:		Thumb Print:

Service Performed	Identification	ID Number:	Issued by:	Signature:	
☐ Acknowledgement	☐ ID Card				
☐ Jurat	☐ Driver's License	Issued Date:	Expiration Date:		
☐ Oath	☐ Passport	/ /	/ /		
Other:	☐ Credible Witness	Document Date:	Notary Fee:	Travel Fee:	
	☐ Known Personally	/ /			
	☐ _____				

Document Type:	Date/Time Notarized: / /	: AM
		: PM

Witness Full NAME: 1	Signature:	Phone No:
Address:		Email:

Witness Full NAME: 2	Signature:	Phone No:
Address:		Email:

Notes:

Made in the USA
Coppell, TX
14 October 2024

38647569R10057